# Tonya Joyner Scott

## Contributors

Iretha Alston
Debbie Baxter
Jenelle Flythe-Brownlow
Katonya Freeman
Roz A. Gee
Charniece Harris
Carolyn Hunter
Beverly Knox Davis
Tramaine McNeal-Wimbush
Christina Mial
Kimberly Mills
Rashonda Moore
Donna Morris Cox
Kelonyee Sloan
Renee Summers
Lisa Thomas-Lewis
Detra Tyler
Letesha Williams
Nettie Williams

*Shine* © 2020 by Tonya Joyner Scott

ISBN: 978-1-64786-896-3

**Cover Photo Credit:** Tailiah Breon

# CONTENTS

# FOREWORD

## Tonya Joyner Scott

When the text message came through asking if I was available within the hour to talk, I was excited and anxious at the same time. What in the world did Trevor Otts, Co-founder of Peak Performer Institute and Black CEO, want to speak with me about? I accepted his invitation.

With his impactful tone and wise counsel, he began to tell me to rise up and answer the call within me. You see, throughout my life I've been the listening ear for so many damaged hearts. I've been a shoulder for many to lean on; I've been that voice of life, a smile of hope and sometimes even an embrace of passion to let someone know that she mattered, was loved and sometimes even safe. Helping others realize that being hurt, damaged or broken may be a *fact of their* life, but it holds no substance to the *truth* of who they are. It was Trevor's call that evening that ignited this passion within me to take action and give birth to *"Shine."*

I am known for saying, "Exposure brings closure." This statement is a principle of freedom. The enemy loves to operate in our silence. He holds us captive when we keep things hidden and tucked away in our mind and heart. But what does God say? He reminds us that we are able to overcome by way of His Blood and the word of our own testimony. It is necessary for us to share—for our own healing, but also for the healing of others.

As you read through the pages of this book allowing these Shine Sisters to share a brief summary from a particular time in their life—prepare yourself as you journey with them through personal adversity, trauma, strength and fortitude—all ending with a common thread of releasing and forgiving.

I want you to know what these sisters know. I want you to know your value. I want you to know your strength. I want you to know who you are, and I want you to advance forward in it. Daily. I want you to lock arms with every sister in this book and scream with us that you are light, and that you Shine. Come on. Ready? Let's go…

"I am Light and I Shine!"

Tonya Joyner-Scott
Visionary/Founder of the SHINE Movement

# I REMEMBER WHEN...

## Letesha Williams

# CHAPTER 1

I REMEMBER WAKING UP TO MEN TAKING MY INNOCENCE... FORCING themselves in tight places... with blank faces as tears rolled down mine. I remember when I would see my parents getting high; not understanding how they could blow money on drugs but couldn't buy clothes for my siblings and I.

I remember when the lights were out and we ran extension cords from trailer to trailer; asking neighbors for favors. No guidance... no structure... just a cracked out father and a drunk mother too caught up in their own minds to notice what was happening before their eyes.

I remember when I let a man tell me he loved me so he could get some skin. I remember when I thought it was love because he smiled each time I let him in; depositing images and thoughts that would later bring pain.

I remember days of no sun and just rain; feeling like I was in a never ending storm. Wanting dryness but soaked with worry; would I awake one day and find my parents gone? I worried for my siblings because they were hungry... I was trying to do it all, so they wouldn't worry.

Then came my blessing in the form of a girl—a girl who gave me hope for a better world; a reason to keep fighting when inside I just wanted to die; lost in the midst of my parents high.

I now understand why I had to endure; so that I could be a voice for those unsure. He kept me humble even when I was weak and now gives me the words when I need to speak. It was all necessary—the joy and the pain. I guess that's how I learned to love the rain—it washes away the old and waters the new; the newness of me...the newness of you.

———

THAT KNOCK BECAME ALL TOO FAMILIAR. I KNEW IT WAS HIM. HE gained access with the bottle he knew would distract her. He had a chair he would sit in which faced my room. This was not the face I wanted to see. I would enter the living room with hopes of making it to the kitchen without him reaching for me. Oftentimes, I didn't make it.

He grabbed me as I walked by. I felt my heart drop. He pulled me onto his lap, and I felt him. I guess his stroke wasn't good enough, so I had to do it. My heart was racing, and I was afraid. I didn't want any trouble. I just wanted it to be over so I could go on about my business. I wanted someone to walk in, but no one ever did. All I wanted was to be saved.

I knew I wasn't the only one. He watched all of us, the young girls in the neighborhood. He wasn't the only one who would violate me sexually. I guess word got out and now everyone wanted a piece of me. The more they got high, the more trips made to my room.

I just laid there. Numb.

They did their business and left. I cried.

I had no clue at the time what was going on. I just knew that what I was experiencing couldn't be right, but I had no fight. The men in my environment used all I knew to gain access to me. The attention I desired was only given if I would engage in sexual intercourse with them. I knew I couldn't bring a life into this mess, so I pushed even harder to escape.

I fell victim to another man. He played ball with me. By this time, I was starving for attention. He gave it to me, but it came with a price. I would leave out of the house late nights and have sex with him. I told myself that I'd get away. Those hopes seemed faded once I became pregnant at 14.

What was I going to do? How could I care for a child? I continued to play basketball until my coach and my Health teacher pulled me aside after class. They knew my body was changing, but I was still trying to hide it. I could see the disappointment in their faces. I was on my way to what seemed to be a promising basketball journey. I was top in my class and up for many awards as I neared my eighth grade graduation.

To my surprise, those were rescinded. My teachers told me that I couldn't be the most likely to succeed because I was 14 and pregnant. I was told that I would have to quit school, that I would never amount to anything. The man who was almost twice my age wanted me to abort. What seemed to be a hopeless situation for me, gave me drive. I would not be what they thought. I would succeed.

Despite all of the adversity, I graduated in the top 10% of my class. I would go to school each day with barely three hours of sleep. The responsibility of a child, school, athletics, and holding a job were heavy, but I would not give up. I signed a letter of intent to play college ball, and that afternoon, those teachers apologized for their beliefs. They couldn't believe that through it all, I persevered. They only knew a little and had no idea of all the other things I was facing as I pushed through my high school years. Every day was a struggle, but she was depending on me to make it happen.

I had essentially been parenting since the age of around 9. There were times when I had to make sure that we were okay because my parents were caught up in the drugs. I can remember the times when we depended on the neighbors and others to help us with food, electricity, etc. I didn't understand, but had to protect my siblings. Through it all, I only wanted what was best, but knew that if I wanted different, I would have to get away. I went off to college but left first semester to join the Army.

———

I was able to get away, but the wounds of being used traveled with me. I was out in the world trying to find myself. I was a little girl lost with big responsibilities. I used work as a coping mechanism. I gave myself away countless times, just as they did. I found myself feeling like I was only good for sex. I can remember countless times I would have sex just because they wanted it. I never understood why men only wanted sex from me, so I started dating women. I thought I could save them because no one saved me. I would still have sex with men over the years. I can only imagine the damage I was doing to the man who wanted more, but I couldn't give it. I was so numb. I didn't feel anything, not even when I was raped. I didn't want to have sex with him, but he forced it still. I had no fight in me. I just let him get off like all the others did.

No one knew what I was dealing with. On the outside I seemed to have it all together, but inside I was a wreck. I was so used to being strong that I didn't know how to be weak. I had wounds that I played in and some that I let heal.

It wasn't until I begged God to get me out of a relationship that He started answering all my questions about why I had to go through what I did as a child.

————

One day, I saw my childhood offender and was shook. I turned and ran to my car crying. The young girl who was violated by him felt her heart drop in that moment. It was the first time I had seen him since leaving home as a teenager. He was sitting in the mall watching the girls as they walked by. I knew in that moment that I hadn't forgiven him. I wanted to, but didn't know how. I attended a camp that really opened my eyes to the trauma I had experienced. During the camp, as I sat there crying during the time line project, I was able to release some things that I had shared with no one; the molestation, the rape, the early entrance into parenthood, the lack of parental presence.

My best friend wrote to me on a piece of paper, "You don't need her now. You are surrounded by love." The very next day, I had a fall on my face moment with God. He revealed to me that I can't get what a person doesn't have the capacity to give. This was my first true experience with forgiveness of self. I had seen my offender a few years earlier and wasn't affected by his presence. I spoke to him and could see the shock in his eyes. There was no emotion released from me.

———

EVEN MY PARENTS... I HAD TO FORGIVE THEM. THEY HAD DONE THE best they could with what they knew. They were in something that I didn't understand as a child, but was able to comprehend later. All I wanted was to know that they cared. They couldn't offer me that. They could only give me what they had the capacity to give at that time. Life had sucked them in and they got caught up in a game that yielded many days of being there, but not present. The way they chose to cope left me wanting a love they weren't able to give.

Forgiveness came when these words were released from her mouth, "That's what you were for. I get the drugs and they get you."

I had asked God on many occasions why men only wanted me for sex. In that moment, I knew what the knocks on the door were for. I had been exchanged for the high. As a result, I gave myself away for them to get high. I was subconsciously attracting what I had been exposed to.

As time passed, God began to reveal how those moments shaped my thoughts about me, men, and life. He also showed me my part in it. Forgiving myself was the first step.

# CHAPTER 2

### The Art of Forgiveness

I KNEW I HAD TRULY FORGIVEN HIM WHEN I LAID EYES ON HIM AND felt nothing. There was boldness in my "Good morning," and shock on his face. I knew in that moment he felt shame, but I was free. The freedom was in my forgiveness.

I know it may seem hard to fathom that the woman I am today could endure this, let alone forgive. Forgiveness is defined as," a conscious, deliberate decision to release feelings of resentment or vengeance toward a person or group who has harmed you."

This simply means that forgiveness is a decision to be free. When I heard the words "that's what you were for" part her lips, I made a decision to be free. The question I'd been seeking an answer for was given. In that moment, I could've easily let that keep me bound, but that's not what I wanted. I looked at her, sought clarity in what was released, and after a few tears, I thanked God for the revelation. I was able to move forward without ill feelings towards her and continue my journey of healing old wounds. It's all about perspective.

Over the last few years, God has revealed to me that I must see the heart of a person and not the place they are in. When we repent and ask for forgiveness, He doesn't remind us of our sin, He wipes it clean. I have come to a place of understanding that everyone doesn't want to acknowledge their diseased roots, or they don't know how to. This doesn't mean that they don't want healing. They may not want to put in the work required. Often times, people choose to live in hurt because they have become accustomed to it. It seems much easier to be the victim. I chose freedom, so I had to release the things that had me in bondage. It has allowed me to separate their actions from their heart, just as God does when he forgives us. The peace lies there.

Forgiveness doesn't mean you allow the violations to continue. It simply means you allow your heart to heal from the hurt of them. You can let go of pain and forget it. Set boundaries in order to protect your peace. It is not necessary to remember every detail, but rather the lesson that stemmed from it. The intricate details will surface when it's time for you to walk in your truth and share your testimony. Keep moving forward. True forgiveness has no emotion attached to the offender. You are able to love them past their pain. In loving them, you understand that they have roots that need to be dealt with, and you lift them in prayer.

Love heals and love releases.

# AUTHOR BIO: LETESHA WILLIAMS

Letesha Williams is a Certified Restaurant Trainer who develops leaders For Carrols Corporation. She began her career 17 years ago as an hourly team member and quickly climbed the ladder with great work ethic, a passion for coaching and developing, and hard work. As a leader, she coaches and develops future leaders. Her calm spirit allows her to capture the hearts of those she works with to help them realize their true potential. She is an instructor for Basic Management Training and is one of the most requested trainers in her company.

In her spare time, Letesha uses her writing to help others overcome adversity. Her gift of descriptive writing allows readers to envision and bring to life the words on each page. As Letesha continues to find her voice, she aspires to free others by being a model for forgiveness, displaying God's love, and showing others that they too can overcome any situation. She is the mother of one daughter and grandmother to one grandson.

# A LONG WAY FROM HOME

Christina Mial

# CHAPTER 1

"How in the hell did I end up here?"

I know, I know! If you are reading this, you may or may not know my bio and that I am a pastor. Let me just say, I am not one of those cussing pastors, but if I'm going to share this side of my story with you, I am going to share it truthfully, even at the possibility of receiving a whirlwind of judgmental backlash. I believe you won't be able to get the healing you need if I sugar coat my real-life experiences and don't share my raw truth. So, let me go ahead and warn you, I'm going to be as honest with you as I am with God.

These were the words I was thinking as I was standing outside of my parent's door about to knock and ask for a roll of toilet tissue. While this scenario doesn't sound much like anything—the truth is that this was one of the lowest of the lows. I was at a point in my life where I had to move back in with my parents—I was drowning in debt and this was my only option. To further my humiliation, everything in the house was locked away.

I stood outside that door, counting my breath and summoning up the urge to rap on it with my knuckles. I fought against the irritation I knew would ignite once she responded to my knock with the singsong voice asking, "Who is it?"

*Who else would it be?*

I was broken. I was an empty vessel walking around in a beautifully crafted shell of a person, but what made this struggle more challenging? I was a minister that God used daily to impact hundreds of people.

Sigh.

Even typing this truth, I find myself cringing a little bit at the memory of wondering if I was a hypocrite for telling congregations and audiences alike how able God is while I was living in utter lack.

No, I wasn't. What I told people every day about the Lord—it was true. However, during that period in my life—it just didn't seem true for me. Can you imagine being a woman who could pray Heaven down... the kind of prayers which brought instantaneous results, but when it came to your own life, you wonder if you need to post your picture on a highway billboard to let God know you're still here. Another thing you should know is that I wasn't in my early, mid or late twenties. This was my life as a 40 something year old woman.

I wrote a book a few years ago and, in that book I shared some secrets concerning my life that I once swore to take to the grave. Listen, even if someone had offered me $1,000,000.00 for some of the things that I revealed about my life, I would've turned down the money. But God being the way that He is, and considering He said in Romans 8:28: *"and we know that in all things God works for the good of those that love Him, who have been called according to His purpose."*

Let me be real with you. Lean in right quick. Come real close now.

"I didn't want to hear that." I didn't want to hear another scripture, I didn't want to say another prayer, I didn't want to receive not one more prophecy. I was tired of *knowing* that all things were going to work for my good.

I mean, dang. How many things did He need to gather before He reached my *ALL* capacity? The more I thought about it though, the more I realized there was a battle bigger than myself and what I was going through at that moment. No matter how hard I tried to run from the teachings of His Word so that I could abide in my feelings, my spirit would constantly remind me of a verse that I needed to apply to get through that moment.

My spirit. Ha!

Do you not know that your spirit and your flesh have two different opinions of the direction in which you should take in this thing called life?

Want me to prove it to you?

I'm glad you asked. There is a verse in Matthew 26:41 in which Jesus Himself is talking. He says, *"watch and pray so that you will not fall into temptation. The spirit is willing, but the flesh is weak"* (NIV). Although I have heard this scripture mentioned many times before over the course of my life—this time it hit me a little differently. It was one of those *Say what now, God* moments.

It all began to make sense to me though. See, there were times where I wanted to scream F--- THIS! But in those times, I wouldn't scream anything. I'd remain silent or I would pray. My flesh was battling my spirit for control of my mind. My flesh wanted me to react. My flesh wanted me to just go off and tell the people that birthed me exactly how I felt. And for those that say, but the Bible also tells you to honor your parents, let me stop you now. Yes, it does. It absolutely does. But the thing I absolutely love about scripture is that it doesn't stop at just one verse. If you keep reading, it also says, and I quote, *"fathers, do not provoke your children to anger* [ do not exasperate them to the point of resentment with demands that are trivial or unreasonable or humiliating or abusive; nor by showing favoritism or indifference to any of them], but bring them up  [tenderly, with lovingkindness] *in the discipline and instruction of the Lord"* Ephesians 6:4 (AMP). Now, reading that and knowing that, I can absolutely say that I had been provoked. I had been provoked for a long time.

What throws me though, is that chapter doesn't tell me how to deal with it when I face provocation at the hands of the womb and the seed that bore me. It took me digging a little deeper to find those answers.

But before we go there, let's explore how we got here.

I have been homeless before. The exasperating part is, I had the intelligence and the means to avoid it all, but at that time I was very immature, and not a very good steward over that which had been given to me.

This time though was different.

# CHAPTER 2

IN DECEMBER 2016, I HAD AN EMERGENCY LIFESAVING hysterectomy. I had a condition where my uterus was growing into itself. This discovery however wasn't diagnosed until after the surgery. While the condition wasn't exactly dangerous, there is absolutely nothing about my life that is normal. When I experience something, it is often to the extreme.

Adenomyosis is the medical term for what was wrong with me. Most women that have it, only experience excessive bleeding and debilitating pelvic pain which makes it hard to live a healthy lifestyle. It is also a cause for many women to become anemic. Let me share my unique experience with you. I had to have a blood transfusion of about two units of blood every single month during my cycle.

Every... Single... Month.

I wasn't living at all; I was simply existing. During the days that I bled, I literally laid in bed with only towels covering my mattress and wedged between my legs. Getting up out of bed was such a burden, that I would lay there for hours until I was on the verge of my bladder betraying me and I had to go to relieve myself. When I wasn't on my cycle, I went hard with everything I did. People used to wonder why I would literally try to complete a month's worth of activities in a day. I couldn't explain to them because once I started my menstruation, I would lose valuable time.

Okay, enough of that. You may be wondering why I added that here. Well, remember I told you I was sharing with you what got me to that moment of standing outside the bedroom door to ask for tissue. After my surgery, I was out of work for recovery for six weeks. That is a long time to someone who makes an hourly wage and I had no time left to use for FMLA.

When you are a child and can't wait to be an adult, they don't tell you is that when you have to stop, the world keeps going. The world doesn't care anything about you being sick or suffering a loss. Real Estate companies still want their rent, electric companies still demand their payments, and if you have children, their hunger pains do not go on strike for you to recover.

Trying to stay afloat, I began to sell things off. It lasted for a little while, but it literally became impossible when I was already a month and a half behind on everything. So, with tears in my eyes, I had to go to my parents and tell them that I couldn't do it. I needed help to get on my feet.

They welcomed me. They did. I will give them that. And for a minute I felt like I could breathe and that I would be able to catch my breath.

Ha!

So, I moved in with my parents; me and my two youngest children and a cousin I was fostering. I carried all my emotional baggage, and as little as I could compact down from a three-bedroom home.

Here I am with my overwhelming amount of debt and walking into a situation where I wasn't given the chance to get it together, but where I had to figure out how to pay about $300.00 less than what I had already been paying. Have you ever thought a situation was a blessing, but when you got in it you realized it was just another heartache?

Do you know the shame that comes from looking at and sharing your bank statements and income with someone to show them your situation and they still look at you like, oh well, this is what I need from you?

Have you ever experienced the emotional turmoil of wanting to die but fighting daily just to live? What about the guilt of what you leave behind should you take your own life and the fear of damning yourself to hell for committing suicide? Can you, reading this now, relate to crying out for help in silence? You put a smile on your face, all while pleading with your eyes that someone would see you?

I have always been the strong one in every situation, even when I was considered the weakest link. If that isn't an oxymoron, then I don't know what is! It is crazy because I can look back over my life and see so many instances where I was the one that was always counted out, but simultaneously the one who was always the one everyone counted on.

Even now, I encourage myself as I am writing out this piece of my story for you. You, a reader who I haven't met, and don't know. I write to you and for you to share my pain, my embarrassment, and by the end of this story, my breakthrough.

I don't write for sympathy, but for my victory. I am a firm believer that I overcome by the word of my testimony. Wait. Let me go back. I just did what I hate. I only quoted one half of a Bible verse. I will rephrase that. According to Revelation 12:11, *I am a firm believer that I triumph over the enemy by the Blood of the Lamb and by the word of my testimony.* That blood part is important. Because as I already mentioned, my flesh sometimes be ready to set it off! It is the blood which covers my spirit and gives me my want to. I think I got side-tracked again.

Let me go back to the story. How many times have I said that? If you are laughing, it's okay. I just laughed at myself in this moment.

When I was a little girl. I knew I was different. I knew it, but I didn't know how to convey it. I didn't know what to do with what I had on the inside of me, so I expressed it every way that I knew how. Let me say this, I was the firstborn child and on my mother's side of the family I was the first grandchild. There are some huge expectations that come with being the first. Also, with being the first, you are the child that your parents don't exactly know what they are doing with. You are the guinea pig in addition to the example. But it also comes with the burdens of not only the mistakes you would make, but the mistakes that were made before you.

I remember a few months ago, while attending Tonya Joyner Scott's "Conversation Camp," hearing someone say that she knew she was hated while in the womb. I didn't say it then, but I could relate to that moment more than anything else that was said. I pretended that I didn't know there were some hidden ill feelings towards me. I remember reading my mother's high school memory book and noting that my name had been chosen a year before I was conceived. I remember the drawings etched of the life she and my father would have, and for much of that, I was included.

But somewhere between the dream of her baby girl being born, and actually arriving, there was a shift in her mindset towards me. My late grandmother used to tell me stories of how I was treated that I clearly either was too young to remember or as a child, my defense mechanisms hid them from me to protect me. I think my earliest memories of feeling unliked started at five. A lot of things start at five. The first time I remember being touched inappropriately and the tingly feeling that came with it was at age five. The first time I became a mother started at five. Yes, you read that right. I was a mother at five. My little sister was born four years, eleven months, and twenty-six days after I made my own earthly debut. From the moment she was born, she was my baby—I hated that she was there and I hated even more that I had to help take care of her. My grandmother said my mom used to drop us off and she would look out the window at me coming in the house with a baby on one hip and a diaper bag on the other.

That was the beginning of me resenting my sisters (because more followed) and me also recognizing that they were treated differently from me.

Why is it that people think because you can recognize something, that means you accept it?

Why is it that people think because you want to talk about what happened to you—it means you are holding on to it?

You will see what I mean by that a little later. Well, maybe not too much later, but you will see.

Even now, as I recognize that talking about the woes in your life, especially if they were brought on because of the actions of another is not easy. It is necessary.

I have lived my whole life witnessing and believing that my sisters were the favorites. I have witnessed them win in areas I lost; all because of how differently my parents treated us. It wasn't until the past year, that they voiced to me that they see it and that it actually grieves them too, but this doesn't make me feel better.

When we were children, if I got in trouble, my punishment in addition to a whooping would often be having things taken from me and given to my sisters. I remember being disruptive in school once and the principal had to call my mom. I got a beating for sure, but she followed up by emptying my piggy bank out and depositing its contents into my sister's bank.

Like why?

There was another time, when I was a teenager and I left the dish water in the sink after doing the dishes and my mother came in and held my head under the water to show me that if I had just drained the water in the first place, there wouldn't have been any water for her to dunk me in.

Before I had a chance to heal from the childhood trauma of all I went through, I still had to live it in my adult years. So, if you can imagine, I had a very hard shell that God had to crack through to get me to the place where I could talk about all this without rage.

I look at the families not only on television, but that I know personally and often find myself wishing that we had that. I wish we had the family dinners, movie and game nights, and meetings to just talk it out like I see others doing, But that is not my reality, and as long as I held on to what I wished I could have, I would have remained in this state of brokenness.

It was difficult to accept apologies I would never be given. It was even harder to extend grace to those that were still actively heaping bricks of rejection on the foundation of my heart. I had to get to a place where I could choose to still be that same little girl walking a path of rejection, or I could emerge from the cocoon of my obscurity and blossom into a woman of redemption. I chose the latter.

But it was not easy. It's not easy when you hear things like "you can't expect to come home for free" while witnessing another sister do just that. Not only do you witness that sister come home for *free*, but you see her get herself together, take all of her money to leave and start over. Then to add insult to injury, you watch the same parent who talked the most junk, turn right around and pay that sister's rent for her, while you are looked upon as less than.

For years, and I mean years, I have carried rejection. Rejection had become my comfort cloak. It went with every outfit of life I wore, and the crazy thing is, no one knew I had it on. I had mastered layering my emotions like carefully laid scarves and adorned my pain as if they were diamonds and pearls.

And then, just like that, I decided to plan a funeral.

# CHAPTER 3

IT WASN'T JUST ANY FUNERAL.

It was the funeral of broken Christina. I decided in order for me to live, she had to die. I couldn't keep holding on to what others weren't doing or how others treated me, especially my parents, to dictate how I was going to live the abundant life that God promised I could have.

So, I decided to kill her. When I began to plot the murder of former me, that is when the heat was turned all the way up!

Allies that I once thought I had, suddenly became my enemies. My finances were attacked more than ever. I went from swimming in a pond of debt to struggling to keep my head up in an ocean of it. I started losing things that I had no preparation to replace. I will give you an example. My teenage daughter's father gifted her with an iPhone on Christmas Day in 2017. He and I had just become friends again just a few years prior. He not only bought her one, but he gave me one too. He said there was a deal or whatever and that he would add me to the account to help me out in addition to his child support payments.

Boom. I accepted that.

I had the number that I had had for the past ten and a half years ported to his account and thought nothing else about it. This man and I had not had a relationship since she were born, so I didn't think there were any strings or anything attached.

I was never so wrong.

Flash forward to June 2019. His new girlfriend gets wind of the fact that my phone is on his account and not only does she report the phones stolen and have them disconnected, but I can't even keep my phone number that I have had all these years. I was so hurt. I couldn't get over the fact that she was intimidated by a ghost, because what he and I were had been dead a long time.

But to make matters even worse, when he did pay his child support for the following month, he deducted the "cost of the phones" that he had given me and my daughter from the payment. Money that I had been counting on to come, didn't come because of someone else's pettiness.

Do you know how inconvenient that is? Do you know how much of a blow that it is to someone that is already in a low state of mind?

I grieved that hit for about a week or two, but then I picked myself up like, *Christina, come on here now. You have been through worse.* And just like that, I ripped up the blueprints of payback that I had drafted up and decided to let vengeance be God's. I reminded him that these things were being done to me without cause and that I trusted Him to handle it better than I ever could.

Wouldn't you know the moment that I gave it all up, I got a phone call to come pick up a phone from an unexpected source and, it was better than the phone that I had lost because of my ex.

Now back to this thing with my parents. A win in one area, didn't diminish the defeat that I was still feeling over this. I had some decisions to make. See, I was still at their house. And I knew that I couldn't walk around living a full life while maintaining a half heart and mindset in my current situation.

So, I made the decision that I was going to do something that I said I would never do again. I made a phone call that I didn't want to make, but if I hadn't made it, it wouldn't have led me in the direction to receive all that I have since and that is coming my way.

I swallowed my pride and fear of what people would say and called the local intake program for a family shelter in the city. I knew that to project my transition, I had to step out on some sho' nuff faith. I knew that there were some doors that would have to be closed for others to be opened, and I also knew for my own health, that I had to get out of that house.

I sat my children down and told them of my decision.

Can you believe that they were happy? They were like "Mama, we would rather you be happy and be your best you than you be content and be only a piece of you."

SAY WHAT NOW?

Now where did they get that strength from? Of course, I asked, and the answer while shocking, shouldn't have surprised me. They said they learned it from me. They said that even when it seemed like they weren't listening, that they were, and that they are always watching me. One of them even said she missed seeing my eyes smile.

Hold on. I just dropped some tears typing that. Let me breathe for a moment. Did that baby really say she missed seeing my eyes smile?

My God!

That was both powerful and pitiful. It was pitiful because you would think by now, I have learned that. I should not think I am hiding anything from those that truly love me.

But here we are, on the cusp of a new adventure. I don't know what the future holds, but I know who holds it. I didn't leave my parent's house angry, but relieved—thrilled that I could walk away before the love died. Delighted that I could walk away before I died completely on the inside. I left knowing that while I can't control what others do to me, I can control how I respond to what they do. I left knowing that there were many things in my past still dictating how I lived my now, but that I had the right to change that and that it is never too late.

Shame wanted me to tell you just a story of what had happened to me, but healing pushed me to tell you a story of what is happening to me. I can tell you this from a place of freedom now. I can tell you that if you are one that has had an estranged relationship with your parents and you try to hold on to some kind of peace based off of the fact that they are your parents, you don't have to do that anymore.

I felt like I could never talk about the issues I was experiencing because so many people that I know have suffered the loss of a parent.

Sometimes when I would tell someone a disagreement that we had, they would respond with "I wish I had my mama to argue with" or "I wish my dad was still here for us to disagree." Those words would cause me to feel guilty. How can I complain about my parents when so many no longer have theirs? But the realization hit me that no matter what they say, it is not healthy to never be able to talk to your parent without arguing. I learned that toxic is toxic and that no matter the source of toxicity, you have the right to decline poison being poured into your spirit.

Rejection is real and it is a feeling that I wouldn't want to impose on anyone. But my trying to make other people feel accepted, was leading me to be neglected.

People love to remind you that our parents can only give us what was given to them. I disagree. They have a choice just as I did and do. I can acknowledge what doesn't work and take steps to fix it. I know that they did what they consider the best they could, but that doesn't take away the damage that was imposed on me along the way. I think there is a saying when you know better you do better. But when someone looks you in the eye and tells you that they are who they are and they will never change, you can't do anything with that now can you? It took a lot of broken pieces for me to find the peace within me, but now that restoration is here, I am going to hold on to it by any means necessary.

I chose me, and it was the best decision I have made in a long time.

I will close with this—I haven't gotten to my next place yet. I pray that by the release of this book I have arrived, so that I can tell you what came after this. I know there are many questions that I may be leaving you with, but for now, let me just tell you this.

I am no longer living as the seed of rejection. I am fully walking in the works of my steps so that they can lead me to the activation of my faith. We know that faith without works is dead, right? When you come to a place where your works means you have to step outside of your comfort zone, are you willing to do so to see faith manifested in every area of your life?

I did! It was the best I could do for myself. Now, although I am in this place physically, I am spiritually alive. My flesh didn't win the battle. My willing spirit is stronger than my weak flesh.

I shared this part of my life because so often, we think we should be along further than we are according to society's standards and we don't speak of our present pains. But look at this quote from the Amplified Version of Psalm 34:19, It says: *"many hardships and perplexing circumstances confront the righteous, but the Lord rescues him from them all."*

Let me elaborate on this as I did in my story. Rescue means an act of saving or being saved from danger or distress. And let's not get it twisted, my situation was truly one of *distress*. The Greek word for release is **luó.** It means to loosen, to dissolve. In the Bible it is used in this way: To loosen, untie, release, to destroy and to break up. God had to rescue me from my mind first, and then he broke up the situation to not only lead me closer to Him, but to allow me to see my worth through His eyes, and not just through the eyes of the ones I loved. And finally, the best part of all of this…

My baby girl just the other day told me out of the blue, "Mama, your eyes are smiling again."

# AUTHOR BIO: CHRISTINA MIAL

Christina Mial made her debut with her Amazon bestseller, *By His Stripes: A Story of Redemption* in 2013. She is the founder of By His Stripes Outreach Ministries, an organization whose main focus is to be the hands and feet of God to those that have hit hard bumps in life. Her other literary works were published under Union Gospel Press, an organization of non-demoninational Christian literature.

Christina resides in North Carolina with her four children where she pastors the NC Campus for Divine Grace Ministries Intl. Christina is recognized nationally for her work as an advocate of domestic violence, being a survivor herself. She has been interviewed on many radio and television programs including Deanna Hamilton's "The Great Mentor." To connect more with Christina, please follow @byhisstripes13 on all social media outlets.

# THE LOVING ME PROJECT

## Beverly Knox Davis

# CHAPTER 1

## The Whisper...

THE DAY I HEARD A STILL SMALL VOICE SAY, "IT IS TIME MY CHILD," everything I thought was going to be my life came to a screeching halt. The voice spoke to me as if a person was standing beside me, whispering, although no one was there. I stood there with an overwhelming sense of empowerment, a renewing and boss babe attitude. I'd waited to hear this voice for quite some time. It was "HER" the one who had been sitting on the shelf, lost in a lifestyle that defined what she had become. The one stuck in a turbulent marriage; in a body that seemed to fight against every gain, and the one who wore both the skirt and the pants. It was a defining moment for change.

After some alone time with God, I realized my marriage was over. The next step was to get a divorce. I had to be strategic because my soon-to-be-ex-husband would never part with his beloved money and would do anything to keep me from successfully raising our children alone.

To add to the long list of my strategic exit planning, This period of my life was the hardest because I had to pretend everything was okay. I had to go about our daily lives as if I was a clueless wife while healing from a partial hysterectomy. The emotional decision to have the procedure was very hard because if the next man in my life wanted children,

I wouldn't be able to give him any. My hormones were all over the map. I was crying in one moment and strong in the next. I was an emotional roller coaster.

Coupled with this was the fact that my husband didn't love me anymore. He no longer found me attractive. It was during my recovery that I discovered he was having an affair.

This came about when a friend shared the details of her husband's cheating. Her marital woes prompted me to check my own marriage. I decided to snoop on my husband's laptop, despite my mother's warning: if you go looking for something—you'll surely find it. She was right.

My ex-husband had been communicating via email with a woman —a woman I knew. I continued searching, despite my heart feeling as if it had been ripped in a million little shards. I discovered that the man I married and vowed to be faithful to until death—had not kept the same promise to me. He had an affair with a woman he met while working on his graduate degree and was emailing a woman he knew from college where he was clearly pushing to have relations with her as well.

I dropped down in the chair as my legs gave way. I screamed as loud as I could as a wave of betrayal and hurt washed over me. I wanted to take his laptop and throw it across the room, but I managed to hold my anger. I had to have a solid plan in place for the sake of my children. I sat there slumped over in pain filled with the rage. I wanted to hurt him as badly as he had hurt me. Was that even possible?

In my quest to know the complete truth, I was determined to crack the code to his phone. My heart sank as I listened to all of the messages left by one of his mistresses. My heart hurt so bad to know the man I trusted, loved, had children with and planned a future with had committed the worst betrayal. It was hard for me to fake our daily routine, but I remained focused on my children and my freedom.

One day, about halfway through my 8-week recovery time, I decided I would take charge and get up from the bed and walk to the other end of the house. I knew this was a challenge, but I just could not lay idle another moment. I got up and took slow, easy steps toward the other end of the house. I felt a rush of pure hatred as I passed a green high back chair—the one he disappeared into every evening while I slaved to cook, care of the children, wash clothes, and prepare for the next day.

I felt like I was a single parent.

There came the moment when my husband forgot his briefcase—I knew it was an accident. He never left home without it. I knew if there was anything else for me to know, it would be inside.

I quickly opened it and begin to read each item enclosed. My heart sank AGAIN! I found statements for a secret bank with questionable transactions, hotel receipts and the receipt for a subscription to a porn website to get a list of women willing to have uncommitted sex. I was even more concerned for my health. Did he use condoms when he was with these women?

I wanted to hurt him so badly, but I couldn't. I imagined him bloodied, and beaten while I stood over him as he pleaded for his life. I had to snap out of that state and stay focused on what was best for my health and my family. I knew it was time for me to make some very smart moves including tests for STD's and HIV. It was difficult to focus as my emotions kept raising so many questions.

*Why did my husband single-handedly destroy our marriage? Wasn't I woman enough for him? When did he stop loving me and why? When did he stop being attracted to me? Why couldn't he give me enough time to heal from having the babies one year a part and to get my body back on track? Why did he break the vows we took before God and all of those people in the church? Just WHY?*

These questions swam around in my head as I struggled to figure out my next move. Not only did I have to protect my children from what was to come—I had to find a way to heal in the process. I also had to find a way to not feel like I'd failed—that I was the reason behind this heartache. I had to reconcile within that none of this was my fault. I still wanted him to hurt like I was hurting, and asked God to remove those feelings. I pleaded with God to mend my broken heart.

# CHAPTER 2

## The Exit Strategy

I MADE COPIES OF EVERYTHING I'D FOUND.

Surprisingly, the pain from my incision subsided quickly as my adrenaline began to flow. It was time to make phone calls, arrangements, seek professional advice on getting out of this violated union. The most important step was staying connected to the Lord despite my hurt and anger. There were days I had so much rage inside of me, I felt like I was going to go crazy. I could not allow my flesh to take over— that part of me yearned to do bodily harm to that man. I had to decide between Jesus and jail. I chose Jesus. It was truly hard to cohabitate with someone who was unfaithful. I knew every word spoken; and every gesture was meaningless.

My heart was sad for my beautiful children. I'd always wanted them to have a mother and a father in our home working together as a team and providing and guiding them into adulthood. I did not have this, even with a mother and father in my home as a child. My dad cheated, lied and physically hurt my mother. It's what I vowed to NEVER have happen in my life. Despite everything, I felt like a failure because my married life began to look and feel like the pain I used to see on my mother's face.

After I was released by my doctor to return to normal activities, I went to see an attorney. It was the season of release of what was no more and to embrace the road ahead as a divorced, single mother.

# CHAPTER 3

## The Attack & The Lies

*The enemy comes only to steal, kill and destroy. I came that they may have life and have it more abundantly.*

*John 10:10 (ESV)*

I CONTINUED TO PRESS FORWARD AND DO WHAT I NEEDED TO DO FOR MY children. One night, while I was in the laundry room finishing the last task of the day before showering and crawling into bed, I felt a presence standing outside of the door.

I looked up and it was my husband asking me, "When are you coming to bed?"

I didn't answer and he walked away. The rage that I felt in that moment. I wanted to rip his head off. He had not done anything to help me with any of the daily tasks so that I could rest my weary body. I could feel my blood pressure rising and knew if I went to bed in the moment, I would have to fight to keep him from forcing himself on me. I took my time finishing the laundry before preparing for bed. How dare he ask me when I was coming to bed just so he could pleasure himself. I felt physically ill; I couldn't bear the thought of him touching me, kissing me and Lord knows... having sex with him. It would have just been sex—no making love because he had violated our marriage with his affairs.

Any other time throughout the day or evening, he was never concerned about my welfare, especially the evenings he came in late from "study" group.

On this evening, I guess he was feeling frisky and I would simply have to do. I literally felt a surge of rage run through my body. He never lifted one finger throughout the evening to help me with any of the chores for the household or the children. I was exhausted.

I took my time getting ready for bed in hopes that he would be asleep by the time I got there, but as soon as I crawled into bed, he reached over to touch me.

Something snapped inside, and I screamed at him. He put his hand over my mouth and tried to force himself on me.

I fought him and cried. All of my screaming and yelling woke up my husband's son who came running into our bedroom. He began to cry and beg for his father to stop.

I could feel my dinner roll up in my throat and jumped from the bed to race to the bathroom to throw up.

My husband demanded that his son leave the room immediately.

As soon as the boy left our room, he appeared in the doorway of our bathroom, watching as I vomited.

"My touching you makes you want to throw up now?"

I didn't respond. I cleaned up and went into the other room to check on the children. His son had gotten his brother and sister and put them in the bed with him to protect them. He was so afraid of his father's actions that it broke my heart. It was definitely time for a serious change. After this incident, my husband and I were like passing ships. Intimacy with my husband was a thing of the past. We coexisted under the same roof but were living very separate lives.

# CHAPTER 4

## The Finale

ONE EVENING, I WAS HOME FINISHING UP WORK FROM MY JOB WHEN AN email came across my laptop. It was from my sister-in-law. I opened the email and grew irritated with each word. My husband had complained to his sister that I wasn't being a good wife. He actually had the nerve to tell her that he was the one caring for the children and taking care of the household. I was furious. Prompted by her brother's lies, she'd fired off a nasty email to me. I responded back to her email, and copied him. When I hit send, I sat back in my desk chair and watched his expression from that damned green chair as he saw the email delivery come across his computer. The look on his face was priceless. He had no words to make it right between us ever again. On top of the infidelity, now he was lying to his relatives to turn them against me.

Enraged, I cursed him repeatedly. I wanted to hit him but I had to think of the children that were already traumatized by his actions the prior evening. I separated myself from him by going to my closet and sitting in the dark.

I felt so alone in the dark in my closet sitting on my stool. In that moment, I just wanted God to give me a way out. I thought about ending it all but the beautiful faces of my children appeared before me and those thoughts immediately vanished. Who would take care of my beautiful babies? One of his whores?

"NO WAY," said the voice inside of me. I was determined to not give in to the enemy and seal my fate with eternal damnation by allowing the enemy to win. I knew God would rescue me, I just didn't know when and I didn't know how.

The next day, when I got to work, I received a call from the security desk to come pick up a package. I went to the security office to find a beautiful bouquet of a dozen red roses and a card. The flowers were from my husband apologizing for misleading his sister. I refused to take the flowers and gave them away.

When I arrived home later that evening, I didn't mention the flowers. I could tell my husband was just waiting for me to say something about his surprise or should I say, *please forgive me gift*. My husband inquired about the roses, to which I responded, "I got them and I gave them away." I expressed to him that sending me flowers at this stage would not fix anything. I walked away to complete my normal evening tasks. The one thing he didn't understand was that his help would have been way better then flowers, him not lying to his family to turn them against me would have been good and NOT CHEATING AND LYING WOULD HAVE BEEN EVEN BETTER.

———

A WEEK LATER, I OVERHEARD A CONVERSATION BETWEEN MY HUSBAND and his sister. She was planning to come visit. I walked into the room to make it clear that she was no longer welcome in my home. He did not heed my words, so when I discovered that she was coming to town, I prepared myself mentally. I was fully prepared for war. Needless to say, the conversation that took place on my porch and into the foyer of our home did not go well.

My sister-in-law stood there in the doorway and I told her she was not welcome. She began to tell me that our home was her brother's home and she was welcome. I apologized to her husband and the children, then proceeded to tell her to get the HELL out of my house before I called the police. I asked my sorry husband to tell his sister the truth in front of everyone, but he simply stood there looking at the floor. I turned to him and said, " I WANT A DIVORCE."

His sister and her family left after I made my announcement. I was devastated that my husband did not defend me and did nothing to keep his meddling sister out of our family affairs.

# CHAPTER 5

## The Call

THE BATTLE BEGAN ONCE MY HUSBAND REALIZED THAT I DECLARED MY intent to divorce him. I asked that we do things civilized for the sake of the children but he was intent on making the transition difficult. The date that we agreed he would move out didn't happen.

The following week I picked the children up from daycare and went directly to my mother's home. We stayed overnight for a peaceful night's rest and returned home the next morning. When we got to the house it appeared that someone had robbed us. The house had been stripped of most of the furniture. I called my brother and his wife to come pick up the children while I handled the situation.

My husband returned to the house with a friend to help. I demanded to know why he was being so hateful. He did not respond. When my husband headed towards the laundry room to take the washer and dryer, I drew the line.

On his final run to the house, he drove up in a new Chrysler 300. He had traded in our minivan for the car. The car needed $1,200 worth of work. I also received a phone call from the mortgage company informing me that the last mortgage payment had been reversed.

I would survive this—I kept telling myself. I was determined.

# CHAPTER 6

## The Victory Lap

THERE WERE MANY TIMES I JUST DIDN'T SEE A WAY OF PAYING ALL THE bills and all that was required to maintain a household. However, God kept showing up right on time—every time I needed him. I would save to make a payment and go online and it would say, "zero balance owed," I would call to make a payment arrangement and there would be no balance due.

I'd go to the mailbox and there would be surprise checks I didn't know were coming. As I look back over my life, and I think things over, I can truly say that I've been blessed, and this is my testimony. My children are headed to college this year and next. We've had a good life sprinkled trials and tribulations—*but GOD*.

My advice, stay true to the still small voice that lives within and never give up. Even in the darkness of your closet, know that God hears you. Trust Him—He will NEVER leave you.

It's my time to shine as I prepare for the empty nester chapter of my life. I have a newfound love in my life and that's ME. Yes, I am able to shine for the light that lives in me. Stay strong and stay the course. Your time to shine is closer than you think.

Blessings!

# AUTHOR BIO: BEVERLY KNOX DAVIS

Minister Beverly Knox Davis was born in Queens, New York but reared in Charlotte, NC. She obtained a BA in Computer Information Systems from North Carolina Central University, a Classroom Management certification from the Children's Ministry Academy and Project Management Professional's Certification from the Project Management Institute. She is an entrepreneur and the proud founder of A Brighter Day – BND Ministries.

Minister Davis has served as a Youth Minister, among countless other roles with the church body. She obtained her Ministerial license in 2018.

She recently received the Mayor's Mentoring Alliance Award in 2018 for Business Partnership of the Year, the Wells Fargo Community Service Award 2018, the Queen City Sisterhood "Women Who's Made It" Award 2019, The Non-Profit Community Service Leader Award by To Serve with Love Ministries in 2019, ACHI Community Leader Award 2019 and was nominated for the Mayor's Mentoring Alliance for Mentor of the Year 2020.

Minister Davis is the proud mother of Ashlyn and Jayden. She aspires to open a Community Life Center in the heart of the neighborhood where she grew up in Charlotte.

For Beverly,
Thank you so
much for your support.
Know your strength
and always remember
to shine!
Enjoy!
Donna Morris Cox

## I AM ENOUGH

### Donna Morris Cox

# INTRODUCTION

I have only just begun to understand and overcome the struggles of my life. I'm torn on how to title this addition. Do I call it, "How to Overcome Low Self-Esteem" or "How Not to Marry Prince Charming," or maybe "How I Survived Six Divorces." Whatever I decide to title it, to understand my choices in life, we have to go back to the beginning…

# CHAPTER ONE

## The Beginning

ONE OF MY EARLIEST MEMORIES I SUPPRESSED FOR ABOUT 15 YEARS. When I was 4 or 5 years old, I was molested by a family friend. I never told anyone what happened back then. He was someone new and really nice to me, so I used to follow him everywhere.

It started with him touching me and ended with him kissing me. I remember feeling as though I was going to choke because his tongue was so big in my small mouth. I told him I had to use the bathroom and ran off. I stayed in the bathroom for so long that my mom came to check on me. The family friend and I weren't in the bedroom very long, but to me it felt like forever. I'm not sure exactly how this has affected my life but I'm sure it has contributed to my low self-esteem. I felt dirty and ugly; like I had done something terrible.

To my family, I'm sorry I haven't shared this with you before now, but I am still uncomfortable talking about it. The truth is that it took another traumatic event to trigger this memory.

While my high school years were fun—it was the summer months that changed me forever. My freshman year, my parents took me with them to visit my sweet Aunt Jamie, Uncle Larson, and my cousins whom I love dearly. Suzanne was like my hero, she was so beautiful, smart, and quick witted. She had a smart mouth, strong opinions, wore lots of makeup, worked as a cocktail waitress, cussed in front of her parents, smoked, drank coffee, and had a boat load of self-confidence. I thought she was amazing, and I wanted to be just like her. Sam and Sonny were like my brothers. I got a taste of freedom during that visit and I hated leaving Franklin, Tennessee.

The following summer, I begged my parents to let me go to Franklin, Tennessee alone. There were no curfews, no restrictions, no calling in—I loved the freedom. Those two weeks were the most memorable and happiest times I had ever had. Jason, who would become my first husband, was a big part of that summer when everything changed.

# CHAPTER TWO

## Husband #1: My Childhood Sweetheart, Sort of...

FOUR DAYS AFTER CHRISTMAS, MY MOTHER'S BIRTHDAY, WE WENT TO bed not knowing our lives were about to turn upside down. Around three a.m., I sat bolt upright in bed like a gun had gone off in my room when the telephone rang, my heart was pounding. My first thought was, "Oh my God, Debbie has been in an accident."

I laid back down and was about to fall asleep again when the phone rang a second time. Immediately, I got up and started getting dressed. Debbie and the entire family had in fact been in an accident. We were informed that two of the 3 girls had died, and we didn't know how my aunt and uncle had fared. They had been hit by a drunk driver.

When we arrived at the first hospital, we were told that Debbie, my best friend and confidante was gone. In addition to her death the older girls, ages 10 and 11, had also died. My 7-year-old cousin had been taken to another hospital, so we traveled there to be with her. I can't put into words, the heaviness we felt as we awaited to find out the fate of Mary. Other than road rash and a couple of scalped places on her head, she was okay. She was instantly mine, heart and soul. I believe with all my heart that she survived that accident for me. Without her, I never would have survived the indescribable loss.

My parents left to check on my Uncle, but I refused to leave Mary's side.

Mary and I developed a bond that would never be broken. We played and we cried as the nurses tried to get the asphalt out of her skin. Because I wouldn't leave her, it was inevitable that I would be the one to answer her questions.

I will never forget that day as long as I live, and it still brings tears to my eyes even now. I was only 19 years old. The Christmas decorations were still up; a big Santa print out taped to the door and stuffed animals everywhere. Mary held on to her favorite, a stuffed Scooby Doo Dog. She was looking out the window and asked me, "Are Sherry and Angel in the hospital, too?" I couldn't bring myself to just say what had happened.

So, I asked, "Do you remember what happened to you?".

Mary said, "Yes, I was in a car wreck."

I said, "They were in the wreck, too."

This tiny, skinny, scared little girl said, "Are they dead?"

I replied, "Yes."

You can't imagine how hard this was, I was trying so hard not to upset her more by crying.

Mary slowly turned her little head, looked at the Santa and asked, "What about my momma?" Her voice trembled as if she already knew the answer.

"She died, too." This was the hardest moment of my life and changed me forever. She didn't cry, she became very quiet and hugged her Scooby. With the weight of the world on both of our shoulders, I held all my emotions inside because I thought it was the right thing to do. I couldn't breathe and wondered how I would carry on.

While in the midst of this tragedy, the memory of my childhood violation came back in vivid living color. It's hard to explain, it wasn't like remembering that time I fell and scraped my knee, it was deeper than that. It was as if every inch of my body remembered what had happened all those years ago. I could feel the touch of his hand on my skin, the smells in the room, his breath, the intrusion, the emotions, his face, his tongue—all this was in my head and I felt dirty all over again.

Mary lived with my parents for three years. I visited her often.

Technically, I called her my sister but emotionally I felt as if she were my daughter.

Despite all that happened, Jason and I struggled to make our marriage work, but I just couldn't get past my feelings of neglect and being taken for granted. I gave up, packed my things and left; thus ending the first of seven marriages.

# CHAPTER THREE

## Husband #2: The Father of my Children

I DID MY JOB TRAINING AT ST. THOMAS HOSPITAL IN NASHVILLE, TN . This is also where I met husband #2.

When I say I fell hard for Bradley, I'm telling you I crashed like a big pile of rocks. I loved him completely and unconditionally. I thought he would make a great dad and I was determined to make him my baby daddy. As much as my parents loved Jason; they hated Bradley.

Bradley and I had a rough ride. His love of women—any and all women didn't help our situation. I would go to his house after work before we lived together and find someone else's panties in the bedroom. My heart would break, why wasn't I enough for him, what had I done wrong. I would get mad and yell and scream and he would lie and make some excuse. I would believe whatever he said, and we would do it all again the next time.

I convinced myself that he was just sowing wild oats and would settle down once we started living together. My love would show him that he didn't need other women. My self-esteem was so low that I felt like his behavior was somehow my fault.

We lived together for two years. During that time, I found panties among other things that belonged to other women. When our marriage failed to change Bradley's horrible behavior, I knew exactly what would fix him. We needed a baby. All I've ever wanted was a happy home, with children and a wonderful husband. I was certain a child would cause Bradley to finally grow up.

Six months into the marriage, I became pregnant with our first child. Bradley was thrilled but it didn't change his behavior. I continued to make excuses for him, and I loved him.

I had an amazing pregnancy, not a day of morning sickness. I loved being pregnant and would pull out my belly for the world to see.

I went into labor at about 10:00 pm on 8/7/88, a Sunday, and delivered at about 4:15am on 8/11/88, a Thursday. After approximately 78 hours of labor, I looked at my son's face, and knew the true meaning of love. All my fears of being a bad mother were washed away by that beautiful face. My son Michael was all that mattered. He was everything and the love I felt and still feel for that boy/man is beyond anything I have ever felt.

While my beautiful red-headed boy thrived, becoming the cutest toddler you've ever seen, Bradley and I continued to have our issues. I decided that having a second child—a little girl was the solution to our troubled marriage.

Once again, I had an amazing pregnancy. Each time I was pregnant, I felt so healthy and I loved having a little person growing in my body. Little Mandy entered the world a lot easier than her brother. Four pushes and she was here.

Bradley continued his drinking and womanizing. I woke up one day realizing that I didn't want my kids exposed to his bad behavior and his terrible choices. I chose to make better choices and moved out to return to my happy place.

Franklin, Tennessee.

# CHAPTER FOUR

## Husband #4: Geronimo

I HEADED BACK TO NASHVILLE WITH A HEAVY HEART. MY MOTHER AND brothers still weren't speaking to me because of my divorce from Bradley this time. From the beginning, they didn't like Bradley but now, because he was the father of my children, he was golden. Even though they were well aware of how Bradley had treated me they felt as though I should suck it up, be a good mother, and push through. I felt like the black sheep of the family. I felt unloved, like no one understood what I had been going through even though I had told them all. Was I not worth being loved? Was I not good enough to go after happiness?

When I was ready to start dating, one of my friends set me up with a friend of hers. Carl was everything Bradley was not; they were totally different in every way and I think that's what drew me to him. Now let me explain something, I said he was different from Bradley, I didn't say those differences were good. Bradley was GQ handsome, Carl had more of a grunge look. Bradley could charm the pants off of anyone, Carl not so much. Bradley was into any and every kind of sports, Carl was into nature. Bradley, never read a book, bought flowers and cards, and wined and dined you. Carl loved poetry, rode horses, hiked the entire Appalachian Trail, took you camping, pointed out everything that was wrong with me, and was absolutely controlling, oh and believed he was Geronimo reincarnated.

In the beginning, it was fun because I was doing a lot of things I had never done before. Short day hikes, lots of camping, horseback riding, and he had amazing stories from his adventures on the Appalachian Trail. He loved the kids and they loved him.

Carl was simultaneously building me up while he was tearing me down. In one breath, he was telling me I was a bad mother and with the next, I needed to build my self-esteem. He told me I was strong and capable even though I wasn't living up to my potential and doing anything right.

Carl was an amazing house painter. He specialized in restoring the old historic homes in Franklin. He was highly sought after and stayed booked on jobs. His dream was to own his own business leading hikers on the trail. He was also a recovering alcoholic and co-dependent.

Carl was given an opportunity to rent a house on a 400-acre farm owned by one of our Senator's family members at the time. We decided to move there together. I absolutely loved the 100+ year old farmhouse and so did the kids.

During this time, I sold my house after many months on the market, so this was a great relief. Carl quit his painting job so that he could start his hiking business. The Appalachian Trial does not run through Nashville and there are no mountains to hike, he was making ZERO dollars. He brought in no money to help with the bills. He just kept telling me how much he would make once he got the business going.

Even though he contributed nothing to the household, Carl had no problems spending "OUR" money. He persuaded me to buy two horses and a pony. It would be so amazing with all the acres to ride and we could get married on horseback. So that's what we did.

After the wedding, Carl continued to spend my house money. He decided it was time to outfit his hiking business and ordered 12 high-end back packs, zero degree sleeping bags, stoves, walking sticks, and every other item 12 people would need to hike in any weather conditions. If I remember correctly, the cost was $8000.00-$9000.00 dollars. We also purchased an acre lot and put a down payment on a double wide trailer. These things, including the horses, pretty much wiped out my savings. I went from being debt-free to owing over $100,000 dollars.

We settled into the trailer and got on with life. I was beginning to realize that I was in an abusive relationship (again), deep into depression, and my self-esteem was at rock bottom. He was mean and ugly, and his words hit me like daggers. His words beat me down as bad, if not worse, than any fist or other weapon could cause. I planned on staying married to him forever, I was not going to divorce again. I accepted my fate and was ready to sleep in the bed I made. My fear was disappointing my mother and failing at another marriage. I couldn't do it; I wouldn't do it.

One day, my mother called out of the blue. She told me that I needed to divorce Carl. I couldn't believe what I was hearing. My family knew that I wasn't happy; they knew that I was depressed and beaten. What I didn't know was that my sister had called my mom to tell her I was in an abusive relationship and it was her fault that I was staying in it.

Even with my mother giving me permission to do what I knew I needed to do, I didn't want to fail again. I didn't want to get divorced for the third time. So, I stayed.

My parents begged me to leave Carl. I told my mother, "If you can find me a mammography position making the money I need to make and if you can find me a place to live, then I will leave Carl and move back to Maryville."

Within a few days, less than a week, my mom called, she had found four mammography jobs close by and a house for me to rent. They had already put the deposit on the house. I told Carl I wanted a divorce and planned my exit.

This is when the real abuse started.

Once Carl realized I was leaving, he put his verbal abuse in overdrive. He even tried to turn my kids against me. Carl was determined to make me believe I was a worthless human and that I would be nothing more.

To cut ties completely, we filed for bankruptcy.

I moved back to Maryville and was getting settled so I had to drive back to Nashville for our court date. The very second, I got out of my car, Carl was in my face begging me to come back to him. When he realized this wasn't going to happen, he became verbally abusive. I went to one of the officers on duty and he refused to help me—just told me to sit down and be quiet or he'd lock us both up. After our turn with the judge, I drove home in tears all the way back to Maryville. But at least that ordeal was done. I never saw him again.

# CHAPTER FIVE

## Husband #4: Going Home Wasn't as Easy as I Thought it Would Be

My idealistic view of going home was not really what I expected. I thought this was going to be great to have my family close by and I wouldn't get lonely. We would do stuff and it would just be a fun time for everyone. Not so much, you see I didn't take into account that they had their own lives and weren't just sitting around waiting to entertain me.

One night, I went out to a club with a girlfriend. We were hanging out, listening to music when she saw a male friend of hers who had a friend with him. I thought Will was a real cutie and charming. What I didn't know was that he was crazy and a con artist who played me like a fiddle. Will manipulated me and persuaded me to marry him within 6 months. Just as quickly as we'd jumped into this marriage—we were divorced 6 months later.

Two weeks after we married, Will quit his job to become a professional fisherman. He had no boat, no gear, and no money. It's a very expensive hobby.

After being married for 6 months, Will called to inform me he needed $300.00 for a fishing tournament. I explained the need for him to get a job because I wasn't giving him a dime. The conversation that followed went something like this;

Will said, "Well I might as well take this gun and kill myself!"

I replied, "Where are my kids?" I knew it was time for them to be home.

He said, "They're getting off the bus now." I told him my dad would be there in five minutes to pick them up.

When my father arrived, Will was gone and so were my kids. I immediately called the police. We had no idea if Will had a gun on him —this man was insane. I was sick with fear.

The police found Will driving around pretty quickly and began following him as he drove around in my van, with my kids in tow. I had never been more frightened in my entire life. The police didn't want to stop him because we didn't know if he'd hurt the kids. Technically he hadn't broken any laws, so they had no reason to stop him.

That day, I was on the phone for almost two hours with the 911 operator. I listened as she continued to keep me informed of where he was and what he was doing. It seemed like an eternity.

Finally, Will pulled up outside my work and I immediately headed out to get my kids. Thankfully, my co-workers stopped me and went out first and brought Mandy in to me. I can't tell you how relieved I was to have her in my arms, but I still had Michael outside with Will. As my co-worker headed out to get Michael, he came running in with a message from Will. He wanted to see me outside. By the time I got to the door, Will had left in my van and I never saw him again.

The police escorted me back to my house so that I could get some things for me and the children. I was grateful they kept Will in the other room, so I didn't have to see him. The house and the car were both in my name but because he had possession of them, I had to leave. They would not allow me to take my only car. So instead of making him stranded, I was at my parent's house without a car.

After waiting several days, I took a friend and went by the house. We weren't going to stop if he was there, but he wasn't. We entered the house to find a mess—the house looked like a crime scene on tv. Will cooked up a bunch of food, messing up every dish in the kitchen. He broke things that meant a lot to me. Will had left all the doors and windows open so the flies and maggots had infested the kitchen. I took lots of photos and applied a permanent order of protection against Will.

# CHAPTER SIX

## Husband #5: Not my Best Friend!

BEING ALONE WAS REALLY DIFFICULT FOR ME. I DIDN'T LIKE MYSELF enough to enjoy my own company. I dated and had fun with my friends; I spent valuable time with my family especially with my father, but it just wasn't enough.

I had a really good friend; James and we had a lot in common. We were happy together and had both been through multiple marriages, both failing miserably at love, so we decided to just throw away conventional methods and just get married. The following couple of years were fine, until another tragedy hit my life full force.

I'll never forget it; I was in the kitchen cooking dinner when my parents walked in. Mom announced that they'd gotten the results of my father's CT scan without preamble.

"Yeah, he hasn't been feeling well and we got the results today. Your dad has pancreatic cancer."

She said it just like that. Since I had been a radiation therapy tech, I knew this was a death sentence. I talked to James and asked him if I could quit my job so that I could spend more time with my dad and help mom take care of him. He agreed.

The next day I turned in my notice.

I think it was five days or so after I quit my job that James came to me and said we needed to talk. He said, "You have been nothing but a basket case since you found out your dad is dying. You're only going to get worse as he gets worse. I can't handle it. This marriage is over."

My marriage to my best friend ended the same month I found out my dad was dying.

Daddy died that year the week before Thanksgiving and the week before my parent's 45th wedding anniversary. By the time he died, I was ready to let him go. I hate that Daddy saw me at my worst but wasn't here to see me at my best.

# CHAPTER SEVEN

## Husband #6: I Thought He'd Never Leave

THANK GOD FOR MY NEWFOUND STRENGTH, I WOULD NEED IT TO survive with my sanity after husband number six.

Depression became a regular visitor in my life. I spent so many nights crying myself to sleep. About a year after we said goodbye to my dad, my mother and I decided to purchase a house together.

One day while shopping, a strange man came up to me and started a conversation. My first thought was, *Oh, my gosh, I'm getting hit on at Walmart. This can't be happening.* Que major eye roll.

Brian was cute, and he came running back a few minutes later. He had chased down an employee to get a pen and was asking for my number. I told him that he could give me his. I wasn't sure if I was going call but against my better judgement I did.

The first time I called Brian, he said hello and then hung up on me.

Maybe that was God trying to tell me something, I don't know, if it was, I didn't get the message he was laying down.

I waited 30 minutes and called him back. Evidently, I was getting some bad vibes that I obviously continued to ignore.

I did something during that phone call that I never had done before, I took notes. Somehow, I was afraid he was a liar and I wanted to remember what he said so I could refer back.

Brian and I married too soon, and I realized that within the next month and spent the next five years trying to get rid of him. Brian wasn't a typical alcoholic, he was a RAGING Alcoholic.

I was at a point where I felt like my life was just one mistake followed by another failure, followed by another mistake and another failure. I felt down, I felt doomed to a life of misery, my life sucked and that was just the way it was meant to be. Was I being punished for the past sins of another life? Was I being tested to see just how much crap I could live with before I completely fell apart?

Another torturous year went by with this man that I now hated to my core. Around Thanksgiving, I kicked Brian out again for about the 5th or 6th time on Thanksgiving and I swore I would not let him back this time.

Another tragic event took place. The day after Thanksgiving my youngest brother died of a massive heart attack. He was 47 years. Brian was able to slither back into my life because I was vulnerable after my brother's death. However, it didn't take long to have him out again. This time I made him pack up his things, furniture and all to take with him.

A month later, he called again to tell me he was getting married and this was my last chance to get him back. Say the word and he wouldn't go through with the wedding.

I hung up on him. He could become someone else's problem. Thank you, sweet Jesus.

This was the only divorce that I can say truly made be happy. I was relieved to have him out of my life.

# CHAPTER EIGHT

## Husband #7: I Finally Got it Right!

I JOINED A DATING SITE JUST TO FIND A COMPANION. I WANTED someone to do things with: have dinner, see a movie, etc. There were a lot of first dates, a lot.

Talking on the phone is something I have never enjoyed. But when the last guy online reached out to me, I gave him my number. When Nick called me, I was thinking ok one more weirdo to contend with and then I'm done with the online dating. That night we talked for over 3 hours, something neither of us had ever done or believed we would ever do. It was a great conversation, we found that we had a lot in common. We laughed and talked as though we had known each other for a long time. Nick was scheduled to go out of town the next week, so he was going to call me when he got back.

Finally, he called four months later, and I had no idea who he was. He'd lost my number but called as soon as he found it. We spent three hours on the phone that night and fell right back into the easy conversation we had started before.

Our first date was August the 15th 2009. We discovered that when he was a young adult, we lived one street over from each other and that he frequently jogged down my street. Our paths seemed to be crossing over and over again. When the night was almost over, he showed me pictures of his two daughters and his son and I said, "OMG that's April. I have a picture of her on my coffee table." We were both blown away.

Both Mandy and April had been on the same cheerleading squad and Nick and I had both attended every game and homecoming event they had ever participated in. I remember all of his kids, his ex-wife, his parents everyone. I also remember some guy with a goofy laugh in the stands watching the cheerleaders and game. Our paths crossed over and over again, until we made the choices that finally led us to each other.

He took me home that night and I showed him the pictures I had of his kids. His son's picture was on my refrigerator. We made plans to see each other again the next weekend. I walked him to the door, and he kissed me good night. I have to say it was the best first kiss I'd ever had.

Nick called me the next day to see if he could see me sooner and I said yes. From the time we had our first date to the day we got married on May 10th 2010, we had only spent two nights apart.

The first year of our marriage was amazing. No arguments, not tragedies, just smooth sailing. We were and still are great partners. The second year is when the difficulties began. It started out with Alex, Nick's son, totaling the car we had bought him the year before when he graduated high school. Alex had been in some trouble in high school with drugs and now he had gotten drunk and ran into a tree. Thank the good Lord he wasn't hurt, it's a wonder he survived.

Alex was now in college studying law and Nick felt like living without a vehicle for a while would be punishment enough. This was especially stressful because at the time of the accident we were in Maine on vacation. What we didn't know but would discover later is that Alex was hiding a bigger problem.

Nick was an avid softball player and we spent a lot of time at the ball field. He even had his own team called the Bombers. Nick loved his team and teammates and they welcomed me with open arms. One night, Nick tore a ligament in his ankle and would need to have surgery to correct it. Instead of resting and putting his foot up and taking it easy, he took this time off to work like a dog mowing and landscaping.

He soon complained of back problems which led to Nick having to have surgery. He had no choice but to rest. In the meantime, we were still having problems with Alex.

As I mentioned before, he was studying law first at ETSU and then at the University of Tennessee. Nick gave him the money as needed for rent and other necessities. On one occasion, he gave Alex money for rent and books, about $2500 dollars.

It was gone in two days. No rent paid or books purchased. Alex dropped out of school. Unfortunately, he didn't tell us or the school he was dropping out. Approximately $18000 was forfeited because Alex didn't withdraw properly from his classes. Nick confronted Alex on multiple occasions about substance abuse, but he denied he had a problem.

Nick and I always enjoy going to Florida to see the Red Sox for Spring Training. It was a great week which we both really needed. We had ballgames, beach time, and way too much unhealthy food.

Alex would come up with one *get-rich-quick* scheme after another. This time he was selling satellite systems door to door, so he went to Texas or Colorado or who knows where to make his fortune. Alex was able to convince Nick that he was turning over a new leaf and was going to go to Florida to work for the summer.

Nick thought this would be great for Alex; that it would get him away from the bad influences. He let his son borrow his Suburban so that he could get there safely. What we didn't know at the time was that he was taking a load of drugs to sell with him. Alex and his *buddy* were stopped in Georgia and arrested.

Alex never said a word to his father about the arrest. He forgot that I was his friend on Snapchat and saw his post about what happened. Nick was livid as you can imagine, he just couldn't believe that his son had lied to him.

He made it back home, but we had yet to see Alex.

Nick wanted to make sure Alex was taking care of the Suburban. So much was going on at this time the order of events may be off but at some point, we found out that Alex had been lying to us about the Suburban. When he had been arrested in Georgia, Alex had used the Suburban for bail money for him and his friend. Nick was even more livid.

He was unable to reach Alex on the phone, so he decided to go by his apartment and confront him about all the lies. There was a pretty intense fight.

His stress was at a high level when we went to bed that night. Nick has a very stressful government job that requires him to get up at 4:30 a.m. His alarm went off as usual and he got out of bed, hit the snooze, and crawled back in bed.

Five minutes later, when the alarm went off a second time, he went to get up and couldn't move. I turned off his alarm, I could barely understand what he was saying but figured out he wanted me to help him go back to bed. Nick thought his limbs were asleep, but I knew he'd had had a stroke.

Since John's phone wasn't working and I'd left mine at work, I ran next door to get help. My amazing neighbors helped me get Nick into the car, since he refused to travel by ambulance.

Nick's stroke was massive, his entire left side was paralyzed. Thank God I was able to get him to the hospital in time to reverse the effects of his stroke. After two days in the CCU, Nick was released to come home. He continued to heal with very little side effects of that massive event.

Life is never perfect, but Nick and I have a strong marriage and work through things very well. We support each other no matter what and make it work. I finally have found my rock, I finally have what I have always wanted in a partner, a friend, and husband.

We continued to have issues with Alex who continued to deny he was doing anything other than smoking a little pot. No heavy drugs.

Nick believed him, I did not, I could tell by the way he acted and looked that he was doing far more than pot. That night was the last time Nick ever saw Alex.

We received a phone call in mid-December informing us that Alex had died of an overdose. Again, we had lost someone we love during the holidays. Alex was only 24 years old, at the time of his death. The autopsy report showed that he had been doing hard drugs for so long that he was in congestive heart failure.

It has been three years at the time of this writing, and it is still hard. But Nick and I are a team. We are strong and moving on with life.

# CHAPTER NINE

## A Total Life Change

MY MESSAGE TO YOU THE READER IS THAT THROUGH FAITH, HOPE AND love, you can survive anything.

Never give up.

Dream your dream.

Visualize it.

Claim it—it's waiting for you. You just have to believe.

I don't blame anyone for the choices I've made. Circumstances beyond my control and some due to my personal choices, contributed to making me who I am today and I'm okay with that.

I love me.

Thank you for taking the time to read my story. It's not the end.

# AUTHOR BIO: DONNA MORRIS COX

Donna Morris Cox is a Life Changer representing Total Life Changes. She helps guide, coach and encourage individuals who want to take their health back and lose weight. Donna began her career with TLC in February of 2018. After losing 54 pounds herself, she found early success in the business and was able to quit her full-time accounting job in May that same year. Donna's love for helping others achieve their goals and live happier, healthier lives is her motivation for this type of work.

Donna lives in Maryville, Tennessee, a beautiful small town at the foothills of the Smoky Mountains. When not working she enjoys spending time with her husband John and her adult children, TJ and Julie. Donna is an avid reader enjoying the works of Stephen King, John Saul, Dean Koontz and other authors of suspense.

# MALNOURISHED ROOTS

## Jenelle Flythe-Brownlow

# CHAPTER 1

How does a tree grow and flourish with severed roots? Is it even possible? When its only source of nutrients has been the unsustainable sludge it's been buried in for years. The answer is yes. I am a beautiful rose that bloomed in a darkroom. I planted my roots firmly in Him, and He lifted me up through the concrete. He placed in me many seeds that bore trees full of good fruits. Thorny vines entangled my body, and many weeds tried to overtake my growth, but I survived. This is my compelling, true story. It is the roadmap I used to go from victim to Victory. I went from brokenness to whole and embracing peace.

I lacked a genuine relationship with God because my heart was deeply rooted in rage and pain. Forgiveness was nowhere on my menu after being sexually abused by my mother's husband, emotionally abandoned by my mother, and physically abandoned by my father at the age of 3. My severely dysfunctional childhood deeply influenced many of the negative choices I made, and paths I took as a young woman. I struggled raising my kids because I was still broken from a childhood I had never spoke of or healed from.

I tried to cope and fix me, but until I forgave, it was impossible to heal or to love myself. You cannot give what isn't within you. It was a vicious cycle I stayed trapped in for years. Many victims of sexual abuse, or rape are too ashamed or embarrassed to talk with those they feel close to, let alone seek professional help from a stranger. Just because someone holds a degree or wears a white jacket does not guarantee they will be able to reach you. Sharing the most intimate details of extremely unpleasant experiences with anyone is undoubtedly difficult, and unquestionably even more so with someone who may not even "get you." Even in recovery survivors of rape, incest, and molestation must "sugar coat" the facts to protect the rights of a monster. Our attackers depended on our silence during the act, and they depend on us feeling guilty, ashamed, and embarrassed to keep us quiet for years to come.

The purpose for sharing my story is to guide you to self-heal, forgive, and find peace. I couldn't do that without first walking down that road myself. While you and your story may be unique, you are not alone in the darkness of your thoughts. I can relate to your complicated moods, your trust issues, your rage. Someone cares, I care. If no one else understands you or loves you, I understand you, and I love you.

I was sexually abused by my mother's husband (who we will call Gary), from the ages of 12 to 15. I am not his biological child. My mother was aware of the abuse, allowed it, and remains married to my abuser today. I became pregnant by Gary at the age of 14 and was forced to have an abortion. My mother chose to support her husband after he was formally charged with molesting myself and another minor. She stood by his side through his trial and incarceration, and after he was released from prison. As a child, my mother forced me to maintain a relationship with Gary. Including phone calls at home, and visitations to the prison during his incarceration. That is until the prison learned that I was one of his victims and my mother was told she could no longer bring me to see him. Why would someone need to tell her this?

———

MY NATURAL FATHER PHYSICALLY ABANDONED ME WHEN I WAS THREE years old, once he and my mother separated and divorced. So, when my mother emotionally abandoned me, I felt completely lost. As a child I remember staring into the darkness all night, often, until the sun came back up. Wondering why I was even born? Why bring me here just to leave me? I felt like I had no use, no purpose. The lack of an emotional connection with my mother was far worse. More tragic than losing her to death because I could physically see and hear her every day, but she wasn't "there."

Not for me anyway.

Just knowing that she chose a random guy over protecting her child broke me down to my soul level. I believe the bond between a mother and their child is one of the strongest in this world. It's like your emotional caliper. That bond is what you measure every other bond in your life by. When it's destroyed, especially at a young age, you will battle trust issues with every other relationship in your life. I was asked a few times, "What if your parents apologized to you, or gave you the reason for why this happened?"

To which I responded, "Sorry is for spilling milk on someone's new shirt as you pass by in the hallway, *not* for intentionally destroying someone's life, killing their spirit. There *is no* reason that can justify turning your head the other way and allowing anyone to do whatever they like to your daughter."

There I was. Thirty-six years old, married and raising kids of my own, but I was struggling with questions that had tormented my mind since childhood and plagued me even worse as an adult.

# CHAPTER 2

IN FEBRUARY 2011, I HAD A DEFINING MOMENT. GOD SNATCHED THE rock that I had been hiding under my entire adult life. I had to look in the mirror and *face myself* and put my true character to the test. I could keep living a lie, or accept my past for what it was, deal with the pain and disappointments, be real about all my flaws and imperfections, and start living my life not just existing. As a child, I couldn't discuss "our family secret" and as an adult I avoided the subject at all cost, and acted as if it never happened.

I needed help to release and heal. I decided that I had lived through enough hell. I was determined to spend the rest of my days happy and at peace. No one can help you if they don't know you're hurting, so I put myself into therapy. I chose one on one sessions. I wasn't ready for group sessions yet. As I walked into my counselor's office for the very first time I felt elated for having the courage and the strength for finally being able to admit (especially to myself) that I had been violated; that I didn't have a normal childhood, and that I wasn't crazy. I was ready to be a *Survivor*. I was done being a victim.

I believe that everything happens for a reason (Romans 8:28-31). Before I can move forward, I need to back up just a little to another life altering moment.

Between August 2010, and January 2011, my entire atmosphere completely shifted. God moved a lot of things in place and some out of the way to bring two of my sisters and I together for a conversation. To back up just a bit further, I gave my life to Christ in November 2008. I had always gone to church, but in spring 2010, I began to genuinely seek a genuine relationship with Him, and answers involving my past. Rekindling the relationship between myself, and my oldest sister was the first in a series of events that eventually led to the conversation. The three of us lived hundreds of miles apart, but when God is ready to reveal or expose something, He can literally move heaven and earth to make it happen.

Late in July 2010, my oldest sister whom I hadn't spoken to in several years, contacted me. We talked about nothing, and everything that day for about three and a half hours. Toward the end of our conversation, she commented, "Do you know this is the longest conversation we've have ever had?"

I was speechless. A wave of emotions flooded through me. I was 35 and this was our first *real* conversation. I held the phone up to my ear like *wow*. The realization that as adults, we'd never attempted to have a *normal* relationship, broke my heart.

---

In January 2011, I relocated from MD to NC. My youngest sister was in the car with me talking to my oldest sister on the phone. I listened in horror as she recounted painful memories of abuse. She had been molested from the age of seven to seventeen. I learned that my mother knew she was marrying a pedophile. Part of me had "known" that for a long time, I just wasn't ready to accept it. I had no idea how to process it the first time I heard it said out loud. When it was just in my head it wasn't real yet. Now it was a confirmed fact. I used to give my mother the benefit of the doubt, but I knew that was just wishful thinking because when I got pregnant, she asked me if it was his baby.

Let that marinate.

I would tell myself, "Gary must have some deep, dark secret hanging over her head." There *had to be* a reason for the madness. I mean, "How else could a woman lay down every night next to a man she knew had touched her babies?"

The "fantasy family" I had constructed inside my head was much easier to accept and live with. I thought that I could will my past out of existence, but in that instant, all my suppressed memories came flooding back. Boom, just like that... the bad, the worse, and the ugliest. I tried desperately to block the images out, playing repeatedly through my mind like a PowerPoint presentation. I didn't want to remember or feel the pain. I felt like I was drowning, wishing my breath would just stop flowing though my lungs, or my heart would stop beating.

Looking back today, I realize that I needed to release every one of those experiences and emotions and allow myself to process all the pain, the anger, the shame, the guilt, the silence... every part of my past that was holding me back from my future. *That* release held the key to my mental and emotional freedom. As we continued to talk that night, the same roller coaster of emotions continued to flow through me. Part of me was glad that we were finally being open with each other, but another part of me was completely devastated. Sad, angry, and hurt again all at once. I was fighting the urge to withdraw inside of myself. I could feel my sisters' pain with every word spoken. I am a strong woman, *the rock* amongst us, but I was overwhelmed with emotions that night. Both theirs and my own. I couldn't be there for either of them in that moment, I couldn't even contain *me*.

My younger sister and I talked during the entire eight-hour ride. We talked about things her and my younger brother witnessed as kids. My two younger sisters and my brother are Gary and my mother's natural children. It had never crossed my mind that they might have seen anything. I knew about my oldest sister, and she knew about me, but we never discussed it.

My younger sister shared with me that one afternoon after school her, my brother, my oldest sister, and Gary were playing a board game, and looking at old family pictures. She and my brother went to the kitchen for snacks. When my sister couldn't get the bottle opened, she went to ask her father for help, but couldn't find him. He and my oldest sister had disappeared. She walked down the hallway to his bedroom door and pushed it open. She was shocked to the core as she witnessed her father performing oral sex on his oldest stepdaughter, who lay on the bed, hands covering her face as she sobbed.

Gary got up and struck his own daughter, splitting her lip and knocking the wind out of her. He then picked her up like a little rag doll and rolled her down the hall like a bowling ball. It was difficult to fight back tears and concentrate on the road after that.

I was furious. She said that she had not thought about that day for years. It's funny how the mind works. It really does try to protect you, even from yourself.

She asked me if she or our brother had ever been molested by their father. I told her that I didn't know for sure, but as far as I knew I didn't think so. I assured her that if by chance they had been molested, that I would still love them the same and wouldn't think any less of either of them.

I shared that I'd overheard Gary raping my oldest sister one night when I was in the 5<sup>th</sup> grade. My mother was out of town for whatever reason. I woke up because I heard my sister screaming and crying. Gary was yelling and slapping her around. Eventually he made her leave his bedroom, (which was directly across from my room), and go to the living room, which was at the opposite end of our apartment. I couldn't hear anything after that. My mother wasn't home, and I didn't know what to do.

We were raised in Germany for ten years; I believe on purpose. There was no family to call or run to. I just cried myself back to sleep. I remember sitting in school the entire next day in a daze. The events of the night before echoing through my head. I felt guilty for not helping her, but I didn't know what to do. As parents, we teach our children to tell us if anyone touches them inappropriately, but for a child—it's just not that simple.

You, as a parent must be vigilant and proactive, know your child and ask questions if you notice any changes. Do a little investigating and trust your instincts. Believe your child. Pay attention when your child doesn't want to be around someone. Even if you ask your child directly, they will probably deny it out of shame, or fear of a threat made by their abuser. My oldest sister once told me that Gary asked her to have his baby, and to marry him one day. Just WOW.

I cannot even try to put into words the absolute rage that began to consume me when I got to the house. I have been through some hellacious experiences, and I still whole heartedly believe that God will never put more on you than you can bear. I think sometimes He removes everything, and everyone so that you only have Him to turn to and lean on. To be completely transparent for a moment, my mind was riddled with homicidal thoughts that night.

Amid the confusion, I had to thank God I was no longer in Maryland at that moment. The home I had just moved out of was only a couple of hours away from where my mother and Gary resided. I can remember days I turned on the news to see bizarre shootings executed by "the nice neighbor" or "the quiet co-worker" that nobody ever would have suspected would do such a thing. I don't condone violence, but that could very well have been *me* that night. I am grateful that I know how to call on the name of Jesus. He had hidden me hundreds of miles, and several hours away in North Carolina with my children. I cannot honestly sit here and say that the temptation of lashing out would not have overtaken me. I had time to think, release my rage, pray and allow the Holy Spirit to minister to me. I called on Him and was able to hear His voice. He took the time to come rescue me.

# CHAPTER 3

I WAS 36, AND LIVID. MY HEART TORN TO SHREDS KNOWING THAT OUR mother knew her daughter—her flesh and blood was being raped by her husband, and did nothing about it. I can understand why she turned to drugs, alcohol, and promiscuity to escape her reality.

After that emotionally draining conversation, I paced for hours. When I couldn't feel my legs anymore, I sat in a chair and starred at the same spot on the wall until the sun was rising again. Unspeakable thoughts flashing through my head. I wanted to take a baseball bat and whack it over my mother and Gary's heads.

I stayed awake for three days. I barely ate and didn't move around much except for aimlessly pacing. I had a couple of brief incoherent conversations with my kids. I felt numb, and extremely fragile. I would watch everyone go to bed, listen to them as they slept through the night, then watch the sun rise and watch everyone get back up and begin the next day. Time had become a blur. I was so lost. My heart turned harder than concrete, and ice through my veins. With no constructive outlet, I turned all that negative energy inward. I was self-destructing. Sinking deeper and deeper into a black hole that was growing by leaps and bounds that I almost couldn't find my way out of. I had become a human pressure cooker.

On the third morning I caught a glimpse of myself in the mirror as I stepped into the shower. I could see my entire rib cage. I looked like a poster child for a hunger commercial in a third world country. I had lost almost 15 lbs. in just three days. I was down to 114 lbs. I have never had a weight issue, but I was tiny and looked like I was sick. I got in the shower and had a conversation with God.

Hate will literally eat you alive like a cancer, and I had six children who still needed their mom. They were my reason to keep going. I focused on them to pull myself out of that downward spiral but ultimately, I knew I had to do it for myself. I was struggling with confidence, and self-esteem issues. I needed something "worth it" to focus on right now. I told God it was all too much, and I couldn't handle it on my own

"Help me before I crumble," I pleaded.

I was not yet at the point where I was even close to thinking about forgiveness. Forgiveness and healing come in steps. This was the level I had to start out on for me. I knew I couldn't keep internalizing my pain. "Letting go," is a major part of the healing process. Before you can forgive, YOU must be whole, and at peace. You cannot give what is not inside of you.

Because of what I'd endured, showing affection was not an easy thing for me to do. When my kids were younger, it was easy for me to hug and kiss all over them, but the older they got—it became harder, especially with my boys. I have been told that when you have been sexually abused, you stop growing emotionally and are "stuck" at the age the abuse started. That was interesting to me because right around the age of twelve is when I began to emotionally detach myself from my boys.

I would have to mentally talked myself through the process. I had to tell myself, "Don't jump, don't squirm, don't push them away, and don't yell at them. Accept the hug or kiss and remember to smile. It will all be over in a minute." I had to have that conversation or abandon the gesture. Which I'm sad to say I have done at times when I couldn't talk myself through the process. I think it's partly due to the lack of affection I received growing up, and partly because the affection I did receive was very inappropriate. The huge emotional void inside of me always kept me in self-preservation mode. I knew that my kids wanted and needed affection. I was just not always comfortable with, nor did I know how to give it. I knew how to put walls up, so that's what I mastered. I blocked people out and pushed them away. I didn't realize that in doing so, I was simultaneously blocking love from the people who had been strategically placed by God in my life. People assigned to help me deal with my pain and bitterness, instead of suppressing it. I was always in search for someone, or something to fill the void in me, and take the fear of abandonment away. I didn't realize that I was unconsciously sabotaging my recovery with my own strategies.

Everyone has a demon of choice. Be it drugs, alcohol, sex, self-mutilation, etc. But nothing you turn to will ever truly fill the void. I turned to unhealthy relationships. Every time I opened myself up to someone new and they let me down, the hole in my heart was ripped wider and deeper. I expected that person to walk in shoes they were never meant to wear. I would crawl back inside of myself, but it was getting darker and colder in there. Until I invited Jesus Christ into my heart, developed a genuine relationship with Him, and allowed Him to heal me from the inside out, I was smothering the very people trying to help me. The problem with looking for love when you're hurting is that you see yourself as a victim, and use *"victim"* vocabulary. That stimulates predators to attack you while you are weak and vulnerable. Vulnerability attracts bullies.

I'm not saying you should find a religion. Showing up for church every Sunday morning, or occasionally going to bible study is not enough. You must develop a *relationship* with God. There's a *huge* difference. It took me a few years, and a pastor with the patience of Job, but I finally *"got it."* The moment I stopped looking for *someone* to physically fill my void, and began to lean on God for everything, the hole in my heart began to mend. I won't pretend it's an easy process or say that there are no down days. Some of the lows feel like a total loss, but those are the days you have to fight the hardest to push through.

My younger sister talked about how we pretty much raised ourselves, and how my older sister and I were often left to care for her and my brother. My baby sister wasn't born until after Gary was incarcerated, so she didn't experience growing up in the same atmosphere the rest of us did. I wouldn't wish our childhood on her, or any other child. My mother did not teach us how to be ladies. Things like proper hygiene, how to use feminine products, put on make-up, do our hair, how to dance, date, or even what to look for in a man. I just kind of figured it out along the way as I got older, and from older women in my life that took the time to share their knowledge and wisdom.

A few days later my sister and I discussed a period when she and my brother unquestionably hated me and my older sister. They were repeatedly told that we were the reason that he was in prison. We didn't even have names anymore. We were referred to as *those girls*. During that season, you could have sliced the tension in the air, it was so thick. The climate at our house was always "hot." My older sister and I left the house by the time we turned 19. Once we were gone, their hatred and anger was directed towards my baby sister.

Further into the conversation between myself and my sisters, my oldest sister provided a major piece of the puzzle that had been our lives. It made sense, but also almost cost me my sanity.

My mother condoned the abuse inflicted by her husband and even provided him with an excuse to get away with it. At his court martial at Ft. Dix, NJ, Gary was sentenced to fifteen years at Ft. Leavenworth, but he only served nine of them. The remaining time was shaved off for "good behavior." There was nothing good about the behavior that got him locked up. My mother never faced any formal charges.

Shortly before we moved to Germany, while we were still living in San Antonio, TX, stationed at Fort Sam, Houston. I remember an incident that took place when I was five years old. I'd been outside riding my bike. I had to use the bathroom bad, so I ran into the house. The bathroom door was closed, but I kicked it open due my urgency. Gary had just carried my sister to his bedroom. That day was probably the first time Gary penetrated her. She was bleeding heavily, and had to be rushed to the hospital by ambulance.

My mother wasn't home, so I rode in the car with Gary to the hospital. He and my mother were not married yet. Gary told the hospital that my sister had been riding her bike, flipped over a tall curb, and fell off and hit a rock. I don't think the doctors and nurses believed that story, but this was before child protective services were automatically called on a case like this. My mom arrived. I also had to undergo a complete physical exam that day, with special attention to my vaginal area.

I was told to completely undress and put on a hospital gown. A male orderly knocked on the door to the bathroom I was changing in and asked if I was a male, or female. I didn't know what that meant at the time. I was scared. I thought something was wrong with me. Shortly after the exam, I was asked a lot of questions by different professionals. I felt like I'd done something bad. After some time, we were sent home with my mother and Gary. My sister had to receive several stitches.

My sister revealed that my mother who was a registered nurse had supplied Gary with the story about the bike to relay to the hospital staff. Upon arriving home, Gary sat her down along with my mother and thanked her for not *getting him into trouble*. He then proceeded to tell her that he might not be strong enough to stop what he was doing on his own and that he might need help. My mother basically co-signed on his actions.

It is difficult for me to think of my mother as *"mom"* anymore. I know the Bible says we must honor our mother and father, but this entire situation really tested the weight of my heart. At times, I would reach out and try to rebuild a relationship with her, and other times I wanted nothing to do with either of them.

I have forgiven them, but I am not in a place where I am ready to reconcile either relationship. This is not an easy thing for me to admit, and it's even more difficult to live with on days like Mother's Day, birthdays, and holidays. I just refuse to pretend. The woman I've become will not allow me to live a lie or show fake love. I cannot manufacture feelings just to say we have a relationship, and I cannot give what is not within me.

The Lord requires that I forgive, but reconciliation is a completely different beast. My mother made some dreadful decisions long ago to turn her back on me and my sister over a man. So, I have made some painful decisions not to allow the raw pain associated with her choices to continue to affect my mental health, my emotions, or my life in a negative way. I am simply guarding my heart by design. Toxic is toxic, no matter what title someone has in your life.

# CHAPTER 4

GARY IS NOT MY NATURAL FATHER AND I CHOOSE NOT TO GIVE HIM A title in my life. He lost any respect I had for him years ago, and I'm not required to honor him. We can be in the same room and I can remain civil, even speak and be cordial. I *choose* to no longer give him the power to change my disposition or character with his presence anymore. I took my power back, and that was priceless to me. I no longer shrink back into that 12-year-old little girl at the sight of him anymore.

Upon his release, Gary told my baby sister that he had been in jail for killing someone. I guess that was true in a way, because he had killed my spirit. She was nearly 10 at the time. It amazed me that he would rather have his daughter think he killed someone, than to tell her what kind of monster he really was. My sister eventually found out the truth on her own. One of her classmates came to her one day in school and wanted to know why her father was on the sex offender's registry. She found out online. She came to me shortly after and blurted out, "I know the family secret." I didn't quite know how to respond, or what to say to her. She was still a child, and Gary was her father.

As they got older, and I became more and more distant from family, my kids would ask questions that I don't know how to answer. I didn't want to feel like I was breeding hate, or forcing my kids to deal with adult issues, or like they had to choose sides or cut anyone off. Not telling them was my way of protecting them for a long time. On the other hand, I wanted to tell them, because by not doing so I felt like I was repeating the same cycle by hiding secrets.

By nature, I am warm, loving, and caring but I developed an uncanny ability to turn my feelings off like a water faucet. I learned how to function without emotion, or feelings. That's how I survived my childhood and learned how to protect my heart. To me it was a necessary for self-preservation.

––––––

MY MISGUIDED PAST LED ME TO MAKE MANY POOR CHOICES AS A young woman. I married at the age of nineteen and tolerated unacceptable behavior from my first husband. We got pregnant after we were engaged during my senior year in high school. A couple of years after we got married, I learned that he was a drug addict, an alcoholic, and was always in and out of jail. At that time, we had two boys, and I was pregnant with our third son.

I grew up with "you get married, you stay married." I mean, my mother stayed with her husband through all he had done, so that was the only example I knew. S*tand by your man.* I accepted my husband being extremely controlling and possessive. When I was younger, I thought it was cute. I thought that meant he cared. Being who I am today, I would never have settled for that. I had merely gone from one predator to another.

As the years went on, there were not too many issues my husband and I didn't deal with in our marriage. Compulsive lying, cheating, stealing, drinking, drugging, gambling, and verbal, mental and emotional abuse. My first husband was always on probation, or in jail, and I was always pregnant. He always assumed that if all else failed, a house full of kids would keep us together. I overlooked, and forgave my first husband for many things, but there were a few that finally pushed me to leave. The final thing that broke me was discovering that my husband was having sex with other men. I'm not homophobic at all. Be with whoever makes you happy. But getting married and having five kids *knowing* that you like sex with other men is trifling. You're playing with a lot of innocent lives, and it's much easier for a man that sleeps with other men to transfer STD's to a woman. I absolutely refused to compete with a man.

The atmosphere at our house was a chaotic blend of ordinary daily activities, infused with a routine dose of detestable activities. During this time, I struggled for years with religion because while everything went on at home, we were in church every Sunday. Gary used to read the Bible to us. My thought was that if all this was okay with God, then Jesus was the last person I wanted anything to do with. Over time, I figured out that a relationship with God is what He desires from us, not religion or going to sit in some building every time the doors are open.

By far three of the most difficult experiences transformed into major defining moments in my life, and what God used to break me all the way down then build me back up, stronger and higher than He has ever lifted me.

The first was the night my youngest son was hit by an impaired driver. He was only seven years old. Before then, I'd built such a wall around my heart; I didn't think I had tears left in me. I learned that night that I did. I broke all the way down. He was pronounced dead at the scene, but prayer changes things.

I talk to God just like I talk to people. I told Him I didn't know what He thought I could handle, but I couldn't handle losing my baby. It took forever for the ambulance to arrive at the hospital.

A nurse asked me if the doctor had been in to speak with me yet. I said, "No." She closed the door. One of the state troopers from the scene brought my other kids to the hospital. Then a man in a white coat walked in. I assumed he was the doctor.

When the nurse said, "This is Father…," I lost it. They don't send a priest in to tell you your kid broke their arm. I didn't want to hear my son was gone so I wouldn't let him talk. The nurse took me down to see my baby but warned me he wouldn't look like anything I was used to. His face was huge from swelling and he had developed four blood clots in his head. He wasn't expected to live through the night. The hospital he was at wasn't equipped to do brain surgery on children, but the doctor on call said that my son would not survive being airlifted in his condition. He needed immediate surgery to relieve the pressure in his head and my permission was required.

The surgery was a success, but my son was still in critical condition. He was being taken by helicopter to John's Hopkins in Baltimore, MD. They told me the next 72 hours were crucial and that he might not make it.

He spent the next six months between John Hopkin's and Kennedy Krieger Institute, a rehab for children that come from all over the world, also located in Baltimore, MD. My son lay in a coma for a week and a half. When he regained consciousness, he was in a vegetative state, and completely paralyzed on the right side of his body, which was his dominant side. His father and I were separated, and he was incarcerated at the time, but I still made the decision to quit my job and be by my son's side during his recovery.

We lost our home, our vehicle, and most of our belongings but I didn't care. The only thing I didn't want to lose was my baby boy. In losing everything material, I ironically began to find myself. His doctors told me they were sorry, it was a terrible accident, but this was the best I could hope for the quality of his life. That pissed me off.

They didn't know who my son was, who I was, whose we were. I leaned down and whispered in my son's ear that he would do everything those doctors said he would never do again. I learned patience and perseverance watching my son literally fight for his life. He had to learn to breathe on his own again. Walk, talk, eat, use the bathroom. He was back in diapers. I was constantly torn between being at the hospital with him and home with my other four children. I refused to take the trachea and respiratory care classes because I told his doctors I wasn't taking my baby home with that or his feeding tube.

*God is awesome.*

The day my baby was released, all of that had been removed. He was still in his wheelchair but only for a short while. His lead doctor said she had never seen anyone come back that far, that fast from such traumatic injuries. I knew then that God had other plans for my son's life.

After we found a house, I went straight back to work. Shortly after, my husband and I separated again, and I filed for divorce. I focused on helping my son resume a normal life. I was a mom, an employee and cheerleader for my baby through his rehabilitation and physical therapy sessions. Along the way I met the man who would become husband number two. It didn't take long to figure out he wasn't much different from the kids' father. I became pregnant. I was disappointed with myself because my divorce wasn't final, and we weren't married. Let me tell you something about God, He can correct any situation we put ourselves into. There is obviously nothing wrong with my plumbing. I have six children born naturally. I prayed and asked God to forgive me and to fix the situation.

The following week I had an accident at work and had a miscarriage. Never had one before and haven't had one since. That was like my get out of jail free card—slate wiped clean. Hubby to be and I were living together, and I caught him cheating. It was my house so I kicked him out but couldn't just leave the situation alone. And just like that I was pregnant again. No free pass this time. We were married a couple of months before our daughter was born.

I was basically taking care of husband number two financially. As the years went by, he became more and more abusive, especially physically when he would get drunk. I would pray about our marriage and God Himself told me to break the connection, but my pastor kept telling me to just pray and give it time. I finally got bold enough one morning to tell him I was done, and I meant it.

He left and got drunk all day. He snuck into our home the next morning shortly after three a.m. and tried to take my life by choking me to death. He had threatened violence several times but never actually hit me. I was in our walk-in closet and he grabbed me by my neck and shoved me into the wall. A few seconds later he was behind me pulling me to the floor. He was a lot bigger than me, and a former marine trained to kill with his hands. I told him twice that I couldn't breathe. Then I couldn't anymore. I felt this weakness I had never felt before, which I assumed was my life leaving my body. In that moment there are only two choices. You give in to the feeling and pray you wake up in the hospital. Or you fight with everything you have left in you.

I fought.

He had my body locked up, so I bit into him and shook like a pit bull. Enough that he loosened his grip, and I called for my son who had come home. He's a big boy. He burst into our room to see what was happening. I didn't have much breath in me though. I motioned for him to call 911. My husband was faced with sixteen years for that. He took a plea bargain and got one month of work release and two years of probation. I was so disgusted with our legal system. People get more time for cruelty to animals. That's why women stay in abusive relationships for years. I could never go back to being the woman I was the moment before I almost lost my life. I filed for divorce a few days after that incident and stayed single for a while to take some time to heal.

----

I SHARED ALL THIS TO SAY THAT THERE WILL ALWAYS BE TRIALS AND tests. Real change comes from within, and it all begins with your mindset. There are people who have been through much worse than me, yet they flourish because they *choose* to. You can make excuses, or you can find a way. I decided to find a way. Nothing was given, I worked hard for it. I *earned* it.

The moment I released my pain, anger, resentment, and let go of my bitterness, my true healing began. The brokenness inside of me started to mend. An indescribable peace I had never experienced encompassed me; a gift from our Heavenly Father.

The void… the emptiness…. the black hole that once anchored itself where my heart should have dwelled is now filled with His amazing love. I unleashed the mental and emotional chains that kept me bound for years. I chose to pick up the pieces of my life and rebuild a brand new, better version of Me. It is my desire that every broken vessel be repaired, restored, and rebuilt. Don't view yourself as an archaeologist, but rather an architect designing a brand new YOU.

# AUTHOR BIO: JENELLE FLYTHE-BROWNLOW

Jenelle Flythe-Brownlow is the proud wife of an Amazing husband, Thomas J. Brownlow, and the mother of 6 Beautiful children: Cedric Jr., Andre, Marcus, Jenea, Shamar, and Sarah. She is a successful business woman, a visionary, a person of influence, a motivational speaker, and published author.

Jenelle states, "I have zero college degrees and no formal training. I became a business owner earning 6 figures a year out of sheer will and determination.

Failure was NEVER an option. I fought hard to become the woman you see today. I became strong and independent AFTER I was broken. My worst pain and darkest days lifted me to my highest platform."

Jenelle believes God blessed her generously in the business arena, but her deeper calling and true purpose is to help restore broken vessels, especially those recovering from sexual abuse and domestic violence. To minister to those who *broke the code of silence*. She is here to encourage, uplift, and inspire.

# FROM BITTER TO BETTER

## Debbie Baxter

# CHAPTER 1

As I sit here in my recliner, listening to worship music, many, many thoughts flow through my mind. Looking at where I was, have been, an am now, I am grateful for God's Grace. I was oppressed, depressed, I had low self-esteem, no identity, no voice. I was in an emotional, mental, and somewhat physical mess, deserving love, but constantly getting rejection, until dysfunctional living became my norm. It wasn't the best of anything, but I longed to get it right. Myself and my children lived in this toxic place for 23 years.

I thank God for being able to hear him. I also dealt with thoughts of suicide, as well as attempting it twice, with no success, to God be the glory. God had purpose for me. Years down the line, God gave me strength to repent to my children and I began to seek Him. He connected me to an Amazing woman of God, Apostle Cassandra Sampson, in 2013, and she spoke life into me, this is when I got my voice back.

To tell the truth, I didn't know I had a voice, let alone, the fact that I had lost it and would regain it. I still had to go through many things, but I could now go through as opposed to being stuck. 2013 was a pivotal year for me. God blessed me with my own place, after 23 years of marriage was coming to an end, and simply existing was no longer an option for me. I now was able to walk around with a sense of peace, and tranquility. It is an amazing thing to come to the realization of true liberty, especially when you've been in a place of bondage, except you didn't know that's where you were. God gave me such favor in obtaining my own place, and I was able to move my daughter and her then 2 children into our safe haven.

We got to enjoy that for about one year, then I suffered some financial hardships, which caused us to have to move in with my daughter and her family.

I felt like a failure. I went into a state of depression. It stuck its ugly head up again. I complained and cried to God for a year and a half. I took job at a call center, which I did not like, but had to do something to survive.

Then, one day at work, I became so overwhelmed in my mind, I went to the supervisor, and said, "I can't work here anymore."

I walked all the way to my daughter's house. It was so cold outside, and everything around me seemed to be moving in "matrix mode." I cried the entire way, asking God why was I going through so much hell.

I had sown so many financial seeds, given of my time to the building of the kingdom, sang on praise teams, played the piano keys for different ministries, and this was my reaping? After my short term of working, the light finally went off, and I got the revelation: stop complaining.

Wow!

It was like someone had a bull horn, talking to me. I began to decree my gratitude for what I did have and where I was, rather than where I could have been. I have been through pain, but I also must acknowledge that fact that I have also caused pain.

# CHAPTER 2

THERE WERE TIMES THAT I SHOULD HAVE SPOKEN UP FOR MY CHILDREN, especially seeing the verbal, mental, and emotional abuse imposed on them. Therefore, I had to repent and ask their forgiveness. We saw each other struggle, but my constant now has been to encourage and assist them as best I can and pray for them. They're each so gifted, and it has always been my desire to see each of them walking in their purpose God has ordained for them. I think the drawback for them has been what they saw in our home as it pertains to parents in the ministry, and it drove them away, versus towards God. They heard heated conversations from the bedroom, had to sit in "family talks" for two-three hours repeatedly, hearing the same things, getting yelled at, discouraged, even preached on over the pulpit, it was just so disheartening. We moved them five times to different states, telling them that they were God-inspired relocations.

The instability was rough, but had the moves not taken place, I would not have met so many amazing people whom God placed in my life, each time I was about to give up, literally. Originally, we lived in Louisiana, and moved to Texas, Illinois, Georgia, Washington State, and North Carolina to be exact. God had strategically placed people in each of these states who would help me to literally live... day by day.

I gave my life to God while we lived in Texas, and the ride began shortly after that. I knew nothing of being saved, but I knew my heart was sensitive to God, and He began to speak to me through the prophetic and through God's many chosen vessels that he brought into my life. Listen, it was scary! My then husband (#2), was prophetic, and I gradually began to understand.

# CHAPTER 3

I NEVER FELT THAT I WAS WORTHY OF EVEN BEING SAVED, USED BY GOD or anything! Why? I'm glad you asked. Because of constantly being told that I couldn't. There would be times when I was compared to other people in ministry, gospel artists, and asked "why can't you do it like them?" I'm thinking, I am trying to simply grasp all that is going on first of all, and secondly, I only know how to do it the way God gives it to me. Well, I got tired of hearing that until it discouraged me to a place of just wanting to be silent and sit. However, that didn't happen at that time, but trust me, later down the road it did. 5 states, 5 moves, I got to see a lot in ministry of what to do and what not to do.

So many wives lost their identity, it was sad. Listen, I had people addressing me as the "Bishop's wife." Like I have a name, and identity. Most of the times I would just say yes, and keep it moving. I can remember times when I was so weighed down from verbal abuse, until I was numb. There was a time, we were traveling to Atlanta to a service, I was driving, and this conversation started, which soon turned into an argument.

For the next two and a half hours this went on. I was hurting so bad on the inside and wanted to break down and cry but didn't because my children were with us. I can remember it was like everything went mute. I could see people's lips moving but could not hear a thing. That's how I would cope with it, turn off the volume, as it were. When I walked in the church doors, the Bishop was up giving remarks before he was to start his sermon.

Everything was going in slow motion, or it seemed to be to me. I was headed to my seat, and the Bishop called my name. I was so out of it, I did not even hear him and someone had to literally touch my arm and point me his direction, and he called me up front. I went to the altar, and that man of God began to prophesy to me, and even said, "Don't worry about the argument that took place even on the way here, nor the words that were spoken to you. It was to distract and discourage you, but God wants you to know that he sees your tears and hears your cries, and he's going to use you mightily."

The next thing I knew, they were picking me up off the floor and helping me to my seat. All I could think was that God cared about me. No way this man of God could have known these things—but *God*.

The expression on the face of my husband though was priceless. All those horrible things that were said to me in that car, God exposed them, yet I didn't have to say a word. The Lord literally fought my battle! Ministry caused me some deep wounds. Each time a church was started, (which happened in all 5 states), I was told that it was my fault that each one failed. No one should ever have to carry such a weight on their shoulders, nor minds like I and my children did. Now though it was difficult for us, we were blessed to meet some amazing people, who still to this day are in our lives. For me the most difficult states to move away from were Illinois and Washington State. We had developed some close bonds and deep relationships with friends, their families and ministries. I started to see patterns of that element of control, and isolation. It always started with him not wanting me to have friends.

Then there came the time that God began to use me. I can remember we'd have noon day prayer, and some of our friends/members would join us. One day while in prayer, the Lord told me to tell my husband a particular thing. I said Lord you know I can't do that because he is not going to listen to me because he knows more about the word than me.

God kept speaking to me, and I kept saying no. Then right before we dismissed, one of the minister's looked at me and looked at my husband and said, "Bishop, God told your wife to tell you something."

I stood there with that deer in the headlight look. I then heard God say, "Read a scripture to him, and he will know that I told you to give him this word."

I obeyed. My husband broke down and I got scared.

The minister looked at me and smiled and said, "It's okay. You did what God said, and everything is going to be all right."

Another incident happened when the wife of the pastor of the church we moved to be a part of, came by our home. I was not ready for what was about to come out of her mouth. "Sister Debbie, God told me to come by here to tell you that He loves to hear you pray, so you have to keep praying. He said there is something special when you pray, so don't let nothing or nobody stop nor discourage you. He loves you."

When I tell you, I was living that, "if I hold my peace and let the Lord fight my battle" for real! Things, you think, would have gotten better, to see God send his messengers to your home and confirm you have his approval, even if it's on your spouse, it is a blessing to your home and ministry.

Nope! It was like being in a competition, except I wasn't competing. I was doing as I was being led, but it didn't matter.

———

TIME WENT ON. WE LEFT THE MINISTRY WE WENT TO JOIN, AND WENT on to help my then brother-in-law with his ministry, then that became," I am supposed to have my own ministry." So, we did that to and it failed, by then it was time to move again. Two more states, two more ministries, two more failures. In Washington state, we joined an amazing ministry, which had an awesome music, theatrics, prophetic, youth, and other ministries.

It was great for a season, but then came that time, when the leadership had to go on a trip to Africa and they asked my husband to oversee service that Sunday. The service was awesome. There were three of us who remained on the praise team to sing that Sunday, and my son and another young man were on the keys. When I tell you that God came through on that day, you would have thought there were six of us singing and the band was on point.

The prophetic flowed strong. The altar was packed with people desiring to pray. We soon found out that it was a little too awesome. Leadership returned from Africa, and on that Monday, there was a meeting. I was at work, so my oldest son and my husband went to the meeting.

Long story short. We got the left boot of disfellowship. I didn't understand what happened and I was like Lord, what's really going on? I was told that the hubby had a takeover spirit and the ministry already had Pastors.

We visited other ministries for a while, then he started yet another ministry. We were just tired, my children and I. Basically going through the motions because of being burnt out. I did it for as long as I could, then one day, one of my children got talked to in such a disrespectful way, specifically being told no because I had promised them they could go to the movies, they came in as we were in conversation, and said, "Excuse me, mama. It's almost time for the movie."

He was told, "Stop acting like a b\*\*."

Something on the inside of me just snapped. My insides felt like they were on fire.

I just didn't understand why my child was being addressed in this manner for simply using his manners and making it known to me that it was time to take them to the movies. This moment made me think back to the fact that I'd had two failed marriages.

The first one because of my own fault, but this second one was my payback for the first failure. I was young and kind of foolish when I first got married. My second marriage was a high price to pay. I was left broken and bitter. I began to see myself as a total failure, with no ability to have nor desire something hopeful or wholesome. The crazy thing is that I convinced myself that my path in life was to be one of suffering, not good things, and it began to happen like that.

Each day I would start it off by asking "What craziness is going to happen today?" It was as though when something great did happen, it was scary, and I'd wonder how long that great moment(s) would last before something hurtful would be said, demonstrated, or happen to make null and void the great things. Can you imagine walking around everyday waiting for something bad to happen? That is such a debilitating level of mental, emotional, as well as physical stress to be under.

I carried these feelings for so many years, but what I didn't know is that all of what I had gone through would in later years help me to reach other hurting people. You can't effectively reach people if you've not experienced what it is, you're attempting to console them through or even help them out of.

My breakthrough came while attending a conference, during a time when I had essentially made my mind up that I had had enough of everything, including life itself. I was down and didn't know that I was about to reach a place where I was free to be me. If you don't believe that a song can bring what you need, it can. The song, *Speak Life* by Kim Person is what did it for me. That song reached into the core of my soul and it helped me first to begin thanking God for having kept me, for allowing me to attend the conference, and to for ministering to me right where I was. I had nothing to hide at that point and I was truly grateful to know how much God loved me and had not forgotten about me.

I had so much love in me, but didn't know that I had this incredible ability to love on people, pour out encouragement, and bring the hurting to a place of healing and hopefulness. It was at the darkest point of my life that the sunshine came to not only light up my life, but make me the light, so much that the light of God permeated through me.

I connected and reconnected to some amazing people of God from the past, who spoke life continually into me, encouraged, loved on me, and literally pushed me to achieve all that was is in my heart to achieve. I would say that that it was a true "trials to triumph" moment.

I started seeing myself as God sees me, his beautiful daughter whom He'd placed purpose, destiny, and success in. He let me know that I don't have to exist in anyone's shadow, but rather stand out and be exactly who He has called me to be. The essence of recognizing my identity made the enemy cease and desist.

In other words, he no longer has any rights nor place in my mind, emotions, or soul. I look in the mirror everyday now and I see this amazingly beautiful, gifted, anointed, thriving woman, and vessel of God who is now walking in purpose, making meaningful moves, which are my favorite words. I am doing some of the things that I have longed to do for 20 years or better.

I'm currently working on my CD single release, coming in 2020, and I am a part of this phenomenal group of profound women of Project Shine. I never would have thought that I'd be in this place, at this time in my life, but to God be the glory. I have amazing leaders at my Harvesters Church, Apostle Michael & Prophetess Chaka Khan Collymore who pray for, push, pull, encourage, and chastise me when needed so that I can be the best woman God has ordained for me to be. Has this journey of mine been heart breaking and challenging?

Yes indeed, but what I've learned is that perseverance, even when I wanted to literally give up everything, has brought me to my wealthy and destined place, and this is my time to *Shine*.

# AUTHOR BIO: DEBBIE BAXTER

Debbie J. Baxter is a native of Lecompte, Louisiana. Growing up in a small town, she values the closeness of friends and family. After high school, Debbie attended a trade school; graduated GPN, passed boards, became an LPN, remaining in that field for 25 years. She has since changed careers and currently works at a law firm. She is a part of the Total Life Changes Family, a magnificent health and wellness company.

Debbie is the proud mother of three children, six grandchildren and one great-grandchild. They are the loves of her life and the push that makes her continue to strive, thrive, and succeed.

She has a passion and love for music, which started her on a path at the early age of 12, where she got her first opportunity as the musician for the junior choir of a local church. This passion, over the years has taken her many places, churches, where she has been the musician, choir director, praise and worship leader, and soon to be, Gospel Artist, with her first single, *God Said It*, releasing in 2020.

Follow Debbie on:
Facebook: Debbie J Baxter
Instagram: @dbaxternew
Contact: baxterdj88@gmail.com

# THE GIRL NEXT DOOR

## Renee Summers

# CHAPTER 1

*SHE HAS WHAT I DON'T HAVE, AND I WANT IT. SHE HAS THE DAD I wanted—the father-daughter I craved. She's also pretty and everyone likes her.*

We can all remember someone from our childhood who we wanted to grow up to be like; a movie star, singer, dancer, teacher, or even a neighbor. There were many days as a kid I observed my friend with her family and imagine what life could be like if I were a part of that environment—parents who seemed happy, loving siblings; a family having fun with a spice of sweetness like homemade ice cream. As I grew older, I pondered on the secret of this family model. I wanted so much to be like this girl—I wanted a family like the one she had.

Ten years after high school, I was eagerly shopping for Christmas items when I heard a voice calling my name. It was Tiffany, the girl whose family was my inspiration. She politely inquired how life was going for me. We conversed, trying to recap years in a thirty-minute interval. Tiffany and I exchanged numbers and promised to keep in touch.

Two days later, she called me. During our reminiscing, I confided that I'd always thought her family was the greatest! I confessed that I especially appreciated the relationship she had with her father. Tiffany responded that she felt the same way about mine, shocking me. I never imagined her admiring my family.

She told me that she'd always admired the strength and endurance of my family. Her words shocked me. What I knew to be challenges and struggle—she considered strength.

After a moment of silence, I told Tiffany that I'd sheltered the real deal. I pressed my face closer to the phone and could feel Tiffany listening attentively as I began to embark on the truth of my childhood.

My oldest sister was 13 years older than me; she'd married young and was living in another small rural city. The next sister was nine years older and married as well. I was not close to them because they were building families of their own. And then there was my brother who was six years older. He went to the military after high school.

I didn't have a true relationship with anyone other than my little dog Buzz, a miniature greyhound and extremely skinny whom I loved dearly. I took him everywhere. People would often laugh at him over the way he looked. I could identify with not being accepted as the norm.

Peer acceptance is important to a teen—it was something I lacked. That and my dysfunctional parental unit added to the sadness I felt so many times over the years. My dad contributed greatly to my emotional state. One memory is of watching my dad back his green Ford F-150 with the camper into the driveway. He took his time getting out of the truck, so I went out to join him. I smelled the alcohol on his breath and could see his eyes weak and falling to sleep. I opened the door and pleaded, "Dad, please come in the house."

It was a struggle just for him to nod in response to my pleas. My dad would then climb out the truck gingerly, then stagger across the gravel and into our house. I recalled my next-door neighbor eyeing him, as shame washed over me. In a stupor, Dad would make it to his room to go to sleep off his drunkenness.

In an hour, my mom would be home from work and the arguing would begin. Many times, my mom and I spent our weekends driving to *boot leg* houses searching for my dad. My dad was what is known as a high maintenance alcoholic. He worked hard during the week but wasted his weekends drunk. I spent most of my youth wishing my dad would find other ways to spend his Saturday and Sundays. His activities added to my feelings of abandonment, loneliness and sadness. All I wanted was a childhood with normal parents. I hated every time my dad showed up at home drunk.

One day my parents picked me up from school. When I realized that we weren't headed home, I was curious but didn't ask. In my home, one didn't ask a lot of questions as a child. It simply wasn't allowed.

———

TWO HOURS LATER, WE ARRIVED AT A HOUSE WHERE WE WERE USHERED inside the house. I had no idea why we were here. We sat in this little living room waiting.

What were we waiting for? Who were we waiting for? I wondered.

Suddenly this man walks out and tells my parents to join him in another room.

I was told to stay put until they returned.

I did as I was told and watched their TV with the crooked rabbit ears antenna.

We didn't linger long after they were done with their *appointment*. I recall listening to the them as they vowed to follow the instructions that the man had given them.

# CHAPTER 2

YEARS LATER, THE ONCE REGULAR VISITS TO SEE THAT MAN CAME TO an end.

That's when things began to change. My parents and I traveled to her hometown to visit with family. While there, we went to see this pastor who was rumored to be dynamic. I can still remember sitting on those hard pews, listening as the choir sang. This light-skinned man walked up to the podium and began preaching.

A small lump in my heart formed as he spoke. I could relate to the message when he talked about living a life for the Lord. Although I was a young teenager, I knew that the Lord was real. I just wanted assurance of how my life would change if I really knew HIM.

I glanced at my Dad and studying him as he listened to the pastor. He was really listening, whispering a soft, "Amen" every now and then.

*Deep in my heart I thought for a moment, what if my dad was changing?*

At the end of his sermon, he invited the congregation to come up for prayer. My dad walked up to the front of the church.

I watched in awe as my dad raised his arms and repeated what the pastor said. He had given his life to Christ. Although I didn't quite understand how sincere my dad's commitment would be, I would forever cherish this moment.

My dad made a total one-hundred-and-eighty-degree change for the Lord. He became a loving husband and great father. I finally had my dad in my life. This is my first personal testimony that the Lord can change people.

Although my dad was okay by my first year in high school, all the years prior to that victory left me with shattered emotions and low self-esteem. I compared myself to the girl I most admired who had the father I'd wanted for so many years. I was bullied in school from elementary to high school. People often made jokes about my Asian-slanted eyes.

I grew up in the 60's & 70's where that was not a popular or accepted look in black neighborhoods. It bothered me, but my mom would just brush it off as jealousy. Tiffany never had to deal with stuff like this—she was the pretty one. No one teased Tiffany and she had the long pretty hair, and no one called her names. She had other siblings around her same age. I felt I was ugly and had to pretend I was happy. The only real friends I had, were a few at my church and two at school. I did what I could to avoid conflicts with other people—I didn't want the drama.

During my teenage years, loneliness was a constant companion. I felt ostracized and I hungered for acceptance. In junior high, I tried out for the cheerleading squad. I made the finals but decided not to partici-pate for fear that others would only make fun of me. I had no confidence.

When senior prom time rolled around, I was thrilled when someone invited me to be their date—I was beyond thrilled. After shopping for a dress, I heard from my date. He'd called to apologize because he'd decided to take someone else. I was devastated, hurt and my already low self-esteem plummeted. His rejection made me feel unwanted and unattractive—I believed this was why he'd backed out. He didn't want to be seen with me. Would anyone ever see me as beautiful? I wondered.

That night, I lay in bed filled with disappointment. I was humiliated and embarrassed because I no longer had a date for the prom. I glanced at my senior yearbook. I sat up in bed, grabbed the yearbook and opened it. There was only my name. Not a single picture of me anywhere. I had taken a senior picture but never turned it in to be published. I was not captured in any social activities or group photos. I'd spent all these years in school and by my senior year, *nothing*. I was an emotionally unstable girl. I pondered on the one moment that my dad surrendered his life to the Lord, and it gave me hope that things would get better.

I held my head high when I returned to school on Monday to face the ordeal of having to answer embarrassing questions such as "Why didn't you come to prom or "Girl, I saw your date at the prom with someone else..."

*I can't wait until graduation to get out of this school.*

I had applied to a few colleges, but I didn't have many to select from because I didn't apply myself as well as I could have—my GPA was very low, so I initially decided to attend a local community college for a year, but changed my mind. I applied to a four-year college and was accepted. The recruiter told me that while I didn't have the grades they preferred—he was impressed with the way I presented myself.

———

MY LIFE WAS CHANGING—AT LEAST THIS IS WHAT I THOUGHT AT THE time. Being in college didn't mean people would be different. I had the same drama again. Girls calling me names and saying I was arrogant. I began to block myself off again.

My sophomore year of college I worked at a drive-thru restaurant and there at the check-out window I met a guy who asked for my number. We dated for a couple of years and in my senior year of college I married him.

I graduated from college and then had two children; a daughter and a son. My marriage was a rocky one—I'd married someone who was angry and stubborn. At this point, my life was not looking any better.

One Saturday afternoon, I heard a knock at my door. It was a lady with a flyer, and she said, "Hi, we have a small church around the corner, and I wanted to invite you to bring your kids to the October Festival."

That simple invite turned into 25 years and I am still with this ministry today. But the greatest change came when my pastor was transparent and said he had emotional flaws from the past, low self-esteem and marriage issues. I became very good friends with his wife, our first lady. My pastor took a trip to Atlanta and brought back material and a dynamic ministry called "Intimate Life." I began to understand the spinning glass in my life that held all these emotions.

This was the beginning of my healing. I could see my relationships evolving with hope. However, I would soon discover that the stress and unaddressed emotions bottled up inside me would overflow into my physical world.

I felt a sudden twitch in my face, which was not normal. After a visit to my doctor, I found out I had Bell's palsy, a facial paralysis. This only added to the feelings of insecurity when it came to my looks. I forced myself to go out in public and address my facial paralysis with a smile. I pressed through the public embarrassment dismissing it as a virus that would heal soon. My face eventually healed but my heart still folded.

———

As time passed, I worked intentionally through the step by step program of Intimate Life. I was finally evolving and trying to break through the cocoon. I knew inside there was a butterfly that had not yet formed. I learned that I was not a victim to my past and why I was fixated on my wounds. My thoughts and emotions began to show a passing cloud, a glimpse of deliverance.

I was on the brink of breakthrough towards my powerful promise, when suddenly I was struck a tragic emotional blow. I was walking up a set of stairs when my legs suddenly started cramping.

I scheduled a doctor's appointment.

The physician assistant who saw me that day, had me walk. After her diagnosis, she handed me a pamphlet with the word, *Polymyositis*.

She explained that it was a muscle disease and that I needed to have a biopsy immediately.

I threw the pamphlet back at her in disbelief. My husband and I were purchasing a new home; I had the children—there was too much to be done. This couldn't be happening to me.

My condition was confirmed by another doctor.

This was the worse news and one of the most disappointing days of my life. After everything I'd endured over the years—none of it was enough. Now I would have to endure my a severely weak body; barely able to raise my head, legs or arms. My children were only 10 and 12. How do you fight with no hope?

I could only set my mind to press toward a better day. Once I started taking the medication prescribed, I began to feel better. I was mobile again and living a more normal life. I was back and ready to take on the world.

As time progressed and I got better, my parent's health diminished.

My dad was diagnosed with heart disease and my mom was hospitalized with major aneurysms in her neck and abdomen. I became her caregiver.

# CHAPTER 3

TWO YEARS LATER, MY DAD DIED OF HEART FAILURE WHICH LEFT MY mom depressed. They had been married for 50 years.

Despite my personal health battle, I placed all my time into her. This was probably not a good decision because it was a challenge far beyond what I had bargained for, like a soldier in the middle of a war.

Three years after losing my dad, my mother took her last breath with me in her bedroom in a chair next to her. I laid across her body as it grew cold. It was my daughter who helped me continue to press forward. All my triumphs made me stronger with each victory. I know I have value and I'm surrounded by people who love me, and I love them. I no longer have hidden scars but healed issues. Although my body still needs healing, my heart is healed.

I was soon introduced to an all-natural health product that changed my life. I was 45 pounds overweight, diet out of control and not looking in the mirror because I was not the girl I used to know. I tried the product and it worked. I lost 35 pounds. This great company gave me an opportunity with making more income. I was introduced to a team who really had a heart to help others. The relationships I began to build with these ladies are more than any words could explain. God continues healing me as I bond with entrepreneurs who love God and desire to help others.

There is nothing like release and healing that takes place in the heart. You open an avenue of trust and life to those around you. I was shown clearly from God what I learned from my mom in the way she displayed her love to her grandchildren. It was my desire to create something that honored her love legacy to me. This is how I started my new adventure in helping others.

My brand is *Gramps4Growth*. My mission is to help grandparents understand their purpose. It is to make a S.A.F.E. Place for their grands. The acronyms are:

S – Spiritually

A – Academically

F - Financially

E – Emotionally

As a grandparent we need to pass on values that will long surpass our life. It will empower grandparents to know that they are a trademark with no duplications. It's been a long road with many trials, but I have decided to keep a rocket ship aim. My goal as I continue the journey of living a healed purpose filled life can be summed up in this scripture: Philippians 3:14, (MSG), *Friends, don't get me wrong; By no means do I count myself an expert in all of this, but I've got my eye on the goal, where God is beckoning us onward-to Jesus. I'm off and running, and I'm not turning back.*

As for the girl next door—I no longer have a desire to be like her or envy her lifestyle. I love the woman I've become and I am unapologetically me.

# AUTHOR BIO: RENEE SUMMERS

Renee Summers was born in Greensboro, NC on 30<sup>th</sup> November 1963. She graduated from Dudley Senior High School in Greensboro, NC in 1982. She earned a B.A. degree from Elon University in Psychology & Human Services in 1988.

Renee is passionate about helping grandparents to become the centerpiece for grandchildren to blossom in every area. She is an entrepreneur with her own business in direct sales marketing with Total Life Changes, as well as "Sweet Pearl's Pound Cakes," and Gramps4Growth.

She is the wife of Randy Summers, the mother two dynamic children, and the proud grandmother of two boys, Tyler and Carter.

# BEAUTY FOR ASHES

## Carolyn Hunter

# CHAPTER 1

## Infidelity

DEATH WALKED INTO THE BATHROOM THAT MORNING. I WAS GETTING dressed for work. I can't remember if he said good morning or not, but I do remember him saying, "I had to lock my phone because my boss keeps answering it."

"Why is your boss answering your phone?"

If this man thought I believed him, stupid must have been written across my forehead. He thought he was slick and wouldn't get caught. However, I was on his trail—the only thing is that I was going to have to reap what I'd sown.

He left for work that morning and I continued to dress for work. It was the year of 2013 in the month of May. I'm not sure of the date, but it was the day of our daughter's final band concert. The plan was for both of us to attend the concert after work.

The events of that day went on as they usually did. I left for work, but on this particular day, a heavy burden weighed me down. I was consumed with the fact that my husband had locked his cell phone and I was unable to randomly search through it. Worrying whether he was cheating was an obsession of mine. It was nothing for me to search his pockets or his cell phone. It had gotten so bad at one point that I'd had our home phone line tapped. I loved him but I didn't trust that he'd honor our marriage vows.

Later that evening, I arrived home while he was taking a shower. I noticed his cell phone was on the dining room table. My heart pounded out of my chest and my hands quaked from nervousness as I contemplated breaking into the phone. Working quickly, I tried a series of code numbers. It only took me two attempts to unlock his phone.

He had already deleted his text messages, but I kept searching; I was sure there was a way to undelete them. There were three photographs of a mysterious woman saved in his photos. She was half-dressed in one. In the other two, she was completely naked. Even though I expected it, I was shocked. Unfaithfulness was a character trait that had shown up throughout our relationship. Yet, this was one of the darkest moments in my life.

We had been married 23 years and were parents of two beautiful children. This was the life I'd prayed for: husband, son, daughter, and a house with a six-foot privacy fence. I forwarded all the pictures to my phone. I heard when he turned the shower off and placed his phone back on the dining room table.

The hunt for the mysterious woman was on.

I called my sister and shared what I'd found. She worked with my husband and to my surprise—as it turns out, she also worked with this woman.

I'd known my husband for 31 years, but I recall wishing that I'd never met him. Over the years, the many phone numbers found in his possession fed into my suspicious nature. I'll never forget the day I arrived home with our children when I felt the urge to check the home phone. I picked it up and pressed redial.

On the other end was the voice of a woman I didn't recognize. "Who is this?" I asked.

She hung up the phone.

I called back and she hung up again. Determined, I called the number once again and greeted her by name.

*Silence.*

"Why is my husband calling you?"

She replied, "I don't know."

After an hour-long conversation, I found out he'd been spending time with her for quite a while. As I look back, I can see clearly now. I was so desperate to be loved that I allowed myself to be mistreated, manipulated and misused.

The night of the band concert was wrecked by the truth about my husband. May 2013 was the beginning of the end of my marriage and family as I knew it.

My daughter came home angry because I never showed up for her concert. She stormed into the house disappointed and disgusted with both me and her father. I'd let my obsession with his infidelity keep me from supporting her final band concert before graduation.

———

IT WAS TIME TO CONFRONT MY HUSBAND WITH THE PICTURES. "WHO IS *this*?"

Instead of answering my question, he demanded to know why I'd unlocked his phone. It was clear he'd been caught off guard. Stuttering and searching for words to cover up his mess with more lies, he posed the question a second time.

I cursed him up one side and down the other. I'd trusted him with my life, and he had betrayed me in the worse way. If I was so saved, sanctified, and filled with the Holy Ghost—how in the world did I end up here?

# CHAPTER 2

## The Confrontation

MY HUSBAND'S LOVER WAS ABOUT 25 YEARS YOUNGER THAN HIM. Ironically, he used to come home telling me how his coworkers were cheating on their spouses and here he was—doing the same thing. I didn't think my heart could hurt this much. I'd hoped by now—his cheating was a thing of the past.

When I couldn't get the answers, I wanted from him—I decided to meet this woman face to face. I wanted—no, needed to know everything.

I called her several times, but she wouldn't answer. I texted and left several messages. One day, she finally picked up after I threatened to go to her boss about the sordid ordeal. My husband worked in upper management and company policy didn't allow dating between management and hourly workers. She was also married with children. The conversation opened with me inquiring how the affair began. She told me my husband told her that he wasn't happy in our marriage. She denied having sex with him, but I didn't believe her.

I could see the subtle changes in my husband early on, but I ignored them. I could feel him pulling away from me emotionally.

I was devastated. I was unable to sleep at all. There was a raging storm brewing inside of me. All I could see were the images of her nude body in my head; wondering how many times my husband opened his phone to look at them and the many times he had groped her body.

This nightmare brought me back to when he was caught cheating when we were dating about twenty-eight years ago.

His parents were out of town and he was left to maintain the home. My friend was going to visit his brother who was her boyfriend at that time. She asked` if I wanted to join her. I was all for it because I hadn't seen him that day. We arrived at the home and I rang the doorbell and waited for him to come to the door. So, I walked into the house to find another woman there with him.

In a matter of seconds I totally lost my mind. I jumped on him in sheer and utter rage. I begin hitting him.

He hit me in my head so hard I couldn't see straight. Although I initiated this physical altercation—I was disappointed in him for laying a hand on me. I wasn't the one cheating. I'm not saying I had a right to hit him either, but my actions were those of a girl who was broken-hearted. I struck out in the heat of passion—he was my boyfriend and he was at home with another female. Right or wrong, I lost it.

I made up in my mind I would never see him again. This encounter would shape the future of our relationship. The wall of distrust went up never to come down again. Slowly, bitterness, jealousy, and distrust crept in and fashioned my character traits. At this point, I was faithful to him until I met a special someone who would become a pivotal part of my life.

He was charming with tons of charisma. He made me laugh and I was really attracted to him. He swooned me like fish bait and reeled me in for the kill. I thought two can play this game but my then boyfriend didn't stand a chance. It was game on and I wasn't going to let him beat me at this game. He had no idea that whenever he wasn't at my house—I was out living it up with my secret new man.

# CHAPTER 3

## The Drama Unfolds

As the drama unfolded, I found myself in a place of uncontrolled anger and rage. My heart was so broken I didn't think it could ever be put back together again. I somehow thought guilt would allow her to back off my husband if she knew I had a relationship with God. I couldn't have been more wrong. Although my husband's mistress said she didn't want him, the phone calls and text logs proved otherwise.

They were calling and texting each other like high school teenagers. I sent her several messages through messenger threatening to expose the affair to her husband. She blocked me on social media. I was so desperate to spy on her I created a bogus account to follow her, thus allowing my husband's affair to cripple me and further damage my character. I began to compare myself to her. I focused on her downfalls and flaws to make myself feel better.

I could hear God speaking to me, but I ignored His tugging at my heart. We must be careful how we release words. I literally spoke this woman into my husbands' arms. I would say things like: I know you like lighter skinned women; I know you like thinner women; I know you like younger women. Obviously, she wasn't getting what she needed at home therefore she decided she would succumb to my husband's advances.

During this time, I was angry and bitter. I decided to ride over to the place where they were both employed. I hopped in the Benz and headed to confront her. It was almost time for the shift to end. I parked off company property and like a hawk, I watched every vehicle exiting the parking lot. With no idea the type of car she was driving, I watched intently so as not to miss her. Finally, she drove pass me and immediately I was in hot pursuit of her.

She was headed home and I was about three cars behind her. There was a railroad crossing with a train speeding down the tracks. We were at a standstill.

As we waited, I could see her car moving. She was backing up performing a three-point turn headed back in the opposite direction. She knew I was on her trail. I jumped out of the Mercedes to confront her.

Previously, I went to the copy center and had all the pictures she sent to my husband printed into 8x10 size photos. I threatened my husband that I was going to plaster every one of those pictures all over town so everyone could see the woman who destroyed our family. I wanted to look her in her face and ask her the question, "Why?"

As she came forward in her car, I walked up to her with the pictures in my hand.

She looked as if she had seen a ghost. She never came to a complete stop but continued to move slowly down the road denying ever wanting my husband.

Even though I was operating in disobedience to God; He wouldn't allow me to put my hands on her. I wanted to beat her to a pulp and leave her for dead, but I just couldn't do it. I continued to follow behind her, but she managed to get away from me. However, that confrontation did not stop her from continuing to communicate with my husband.

He begged me to get rid of those pictures. He was busted and he couldn't deny it. He even broke down and cried like a baby. Even his tears were nothing more than lies streaming down his face.

# CHAPTER 4

## What About the Children?

OUR CURRENT CULTURE ACCEPTS BEHAVIOR THAT WAS CONSIDERED socially and morally wrong as a child. My grandmother, a godly woman of great wisdom once told me that if a man laid down and wallowed in the dirt, he would still be the same man and would still be respected. However, if a woman did the same, she would be called every whore in the book. I taught my children many of those same lessons and Biblical principles Grandma instilled in me.

———

MY DAUGHTER WAS 18 WHEN THE WORLD CAME CRASHING DOWN around us. I decided to be honest with her. I felt like she was old enough to be told of her father's infidelity. My heart ached at the look of disappointment I glimpsed in her eyes. I explained that was the reason I'd missed her concert. I showed her the pictures of her father's mistress.

She was a daddy's girl and didn't want to believe her father would do something so degrading to our family. She was in utter disbelief. Our son was away in his second year of college when he got the news. His relationship with his father became estranged. Children are the innocent ones in broken homes, and they don't deserve the things they have to endure at the hands of immature parents.

In hindsight, I could have behaved differently and provided more support to my family. I now take ownership for the things I've done to cause my children pain. Such as sharing things with them that they didn't need to know concerning my husband and me. I did the best I could at the time.

A few weeks went by as we prepared for our daughter's high school graduation. She was excited to be starting her first year in college. She was ready to get away from all the drama in the house between me and her father.

As for me, I was becoming more erratic. I waited for the mail carrier to bring the phone bill so that I could check it for text logs and phone calls between my husband and his mistress. All our cell phones were with one company. We argued constantly because he wanted to go solo with a separate phone carrier. I felt he wanted to do this so that he could have the freedom to talk with her without me getting in the way.

He kept up the lie, saying he was no longer in contact with her, but the phone bill showed something totally different. I eventually called the phone company and had her number blocked so that he couldn't call or text her.

He was livid.

I later created an account online to watch the account more closely. It was obvious he had developed feelings for her. I felt as if I didn't know the man he'd become. I spent too much energy in investigative mode when I should have been praying for my husband and family. I believe that fasting and prayer could have turned this situation around, but I was too busy operating in my flesh and emotions. Matthew 17:21 says, "However, this kind does not go out except by prayer and fasting."

The night of my daughter's graduation, I tried to let go of the resentment I felt toward my husband. I wanted to focus on her special night. Our son was home from college. We were all back together again and it felt good, but there was something missing. We all got dressed up and attended her graduation. We were so proud of her and her accomplishment. We had dreamed of this moment since she was born. There was family support from both sides of the family in attendance.

Where did the time go?

Both of our children are all grown up. No more babies. Becoming an empty nester was surreal. I thank God for the two gifts He entrusted to us to nurture, protect, and raise up to be the beautiful adults they have become to be. I continue to speak encouragement over them. I pray for them. I ask God to cover, shield, and protect them from all hurt, harm, and danger. And allow them to be all He has created them to be.

# CHAPTER 5

## Say You Love Me

I BELIEVE SOMETIMES A MAN'S CHEATING ISN'T ABOUT SEX. A MAN needs to feel respected and appreciated by his woman. I thought by taking care of the children, keeping the house clean, washing clothes, and cooking was all I needed to do to be a good wife. I thought I had those things down to a science. Not realizing I needed to be more than a maid to my husband.

He was studying for his degree and one day while at the table submitting an assignment, he continued to ignore me as he usually did, I asked him, "Do you love me?"

I waited for an answer, then when none was forthcoming, I repeated the question.

He went on with working on his computer as if he didn't hear me.

I asked the question a third time.

He finally looked up and asked me to stop as he usually did. I needed an answer and I wasn't going to stop until he answered my question. I screamed to the top of my lungs, "*Do you love me?*"

I began to throw objects off the dinning room table. The first to go was my beautiful centerpiece which shattered into a million pieces.

I began to pace as my rage intensified.

Our children came running downstairs to see what was going on. I told them, "Your father can't tell me he loves me."

They stood there speechless.

I continued to pace the floor in red hot fury.

You could see fear in his eyes.

He suddenly got up from the table and threatened to call the police if I didn't stop.

I lunged at him before throwing and breaking picture frames which was horrible behavior was witnessed by our children. Both children held me down to keep me from continuously walking on broken glass and attacking him.

My husband called the police and told them I'd assaulted him. It is a dangerous thing to lose yourself in such rage.

My heart dropped to the pit of my stomach when I was ordered me to put my hands behind my back. I couldn't believe the man I'd given my entire life, my love and my body to—he had done this to me. I was placed under arrest for assault and never had the opportunity to tell my side.

I was put into the backseat of the police car as if I was a criminal and escorted to the police department where mug shots were taken of me. This was the most humiliating thing that had ever happened to me. At the age of 50, I was being charged for assault by my own husband. I spent Sunday evening, and part of Monday in lock up. This experience was humbling. I had let go of the hand of God and took matters into my own hands.

I had to sleep on a cold concrete floor in the cell because all the beds were full. There wasn't anywhere to urinate in private. We hung a sheet up for me to have privacy. I met some beautiful women who were also experiencing consequences from negative choices they made. One and a half days in a jail cell was all I could handle.

I did a lot of crying and praying to God. This was one of the lowest points in my life. This valley experience had me wondering how I got to this place in my life. I thought, I'm wife, mother, Minister of the Gospel, and nurse; why am I here? I tried to fight my own battles when God clearly told me that vengeance belonged to Him. I got out of line and suffered major consequences.

On morning of my release, I was escorted to the court room to meet with the judge. I was dressed in an orange jumpsuit with shackles around my ankles and my hair frayed all over my head. I looked up and saw my sisters entering the court room. They were sobbing uncontrollably.

This was the weekend we had planned to take our daughter to her college orientation. Instead our family was complete and utter turmoil. Reservations were already in place to stay in the city where my daughter would be attending college that fall. My husband decided to drive. He and my daughter went without me the first day. I joined them for the last day of orientation after my release.

My husband dropped the assault charges during our first court appearance, but never did he declare his love for me.

I was broken and devastated.

# CHAPTER 6

## Empty Nest

SOME TIME HAD PASSED, AND IT WAS TIME FOR BOTH OF OUR CHILDREN to go off to college. When my husband and I were dating. We sat under the moonlight and talked about the kind life we wanted to live together. We talked about purchasing a home and the number of children we desired.

God granted us our dreams. And as we grew older, we worked hard to achieve new goals and aspirations. We wanted better for our children than we had growing up. I never considered college as an option for myself but was blessed to complete my studies to obtain my license as a nurse. My husband had a real estate license and a degree in information technology.

I was having a really difficult time with becoming an empty nester. However, I hoped maybe my husband and I would grow closer in our relationship. I had forgotten how to enjoy him without our children being around. It was as if we were strangers.

I'd made the decision to further my education and pursue my Registered Nursing degree. I had selflessly put my life on hold to allow my husband and our children to grow. My husband was reluctant toward me going back to school, although he was back in school working toward a degree in homeland security.

Going back to school helped me to cope with missing my children. It allowed me the opportunity to meet new people and focus on personal goals for myself. I felt better about myself and I tried not to worry about what my husband was doing. But in the back of my mind I continuously wondered about his whereabouts when I was in nursing class or in clinicals. I usually gave him a difficult time, accusing him of meeting her behind my back.

I was missing my children tremendously since I didn't have the opportunity to visit them very often. But they always came home for the holidays. I enjoyed those times when my family was together. It felt like old times when there was a sense of love and peace. I didn't realize how much I loved my family until that dreaded day.

# CHAPTER 7

## The Beginning of the End

TIME FLEW SO FAST AND IT WAS NOW APRIL 2014. STILL DRILLING AT the bit and grinding to obtain my associate degree in nursing. On this day in particularly, I was assigned to shadow an RN from a home health agency. We visited three patients in their homes to provide assessments and medication reconciliation. We finished up a bit early so I decided to come home early, curious as to what my husband could be doing.

I arrived home and put the key in the doorknob. I turned it slowly trying not to be heard by him. I turned the knob with hopes he would not hear me entering our home. I could hear his voice in a conversation on the phone. I startled him when I entered the room. He was standing in our bedroom looking in the mirror as he worked out in his underwear while talking on a phone I'd never seen before. I asked him, "Who are you talking to?"

He immediately threw the phone under the bed. We both dived to get the phone. He grabbed it and ran out of the room. I was on his trail.

I throw the artificial plant at him as he brushed by me running to try and get out of the door. I grabbed his tee shirt he was wearing as it ripped, taking skin from his chest.

He ran out of the door and I ran behind him yelling and cursing while trying to catch him. He jumped into his truck and took off down the road.

When he called me, I threatened to go to his job and report his affair to his boss. He had never stopped talking to her. He went as far as to secretly purchase another phone to continue his affair with this woman. I was unaware he was on his way to the police department to take another warrant out on me for assault.

I got in my car and was on my way to his job. My emotions had got the best of me. I wanted him to hurt like I was hurting. It felt like someone had taken a knife and jabbed into the depths of my heart. This was the deepest hurt I'd ever felt in my entire life. He continued with his lies and deceit satisfying the lust of his flesh, lust of his eyes, and the pride of life.

As I rode to his job there were so many thoughts going through my mind. There was a part of me who didn't want to hurt him like he'd hurt me. I didn't want to expose him to his boss that way. But then I let my anger get the best of me. I began to think about all he had done to me and those thoughts were fuel to the fire.

With pictures of her in my hand, I entered his place of employment. Staff members paged his boss to the area where I waited. Although I regretted being there, I informed his supervisor that my husband was having an affair with a coworker, thus violating company policy. My actions did not yield the results I was hoping for—I was escorted off the premises and asked not to come back. My conniving scheme had backfired in my face.

At some point, I felt led to check our joint savings account and discovered he'd transferred all our savings to one of his accounts, leaving me with only a thousand dollars. This was the end of our marriage.

# CHAPTER 8

## Doom & Gloom

A POLICE OFFICER DROVE UP SHORTLY AFTER I RETURNED HOME. HE asked me about the scar on my husband's chest. I wasn't aware I had grabbed him hard enough to leave a scar. My husband kept saying, "I told you not to do it."

I was in rebellion to God and I had to be stopped. I'm not sure what would have happened that night because I wanted to get even no matter the cost. I was arrested a second time, and ordered to get in the police car. The sound of the handcuffs clanging was all too familiar as they clicked around my wrists. My husband sat on the front porch watching.

Overwhelmed with conviction and embarrassment, the process began all over again. I could not believe I'd got myself into this situation again. While on my way to jail, I could make a few phone calls. I called my pastors and my husband. I cried uncontrollably as I made each phone call. This was when I knew I needed God to step into this situation.

I had to be stripped of everything; my clothes, my rings, and even my hair ties. I was given an orange jumpsuit to wear while incarcerated. I didn't think I would ever see those jail cells again. I took my place on the floor with my blanket and sheet. Just like Jesus, there was no room at the inn. I had to sleep on the floor until someone was released the next day. I was allowed my own cell the next night. I tried to make the best out of a terrible situation. The opportunity to minister about Jesus presented itself. I felt like Paul as I shared the love of Jesus while in jail.

While in jail, I had time to ponder on the way everything occurred. I began to have feelings of regret concerning my part in the breakup. I was released on that Monday afternoon. My sisters picked me up to take me home not knowing what I would find when I got there. I wasn't sure where my husband had been the entire weekend. I later found out he went on vacation and stayed at the resort we purchased over 12 years ago. How could he do this?

I found he had removed all his clothes from the closet. His guns were gone along with his fishing rods and reels. Even though I expected this, it still felt like a scene out of a movie. The abandonment I felt was like no other. He'd left me for another woman who was still at home with her husband. Afraid he would come back that evening, my son and I stayed at a local hotel until the next day. I could not believe the man I married had turned his back on the me and the entire family.

# CHAPTER 9

## A New Day

AFTER THE INITIAL SHOCK WORE OFF, I STRUGGLED TO PICK UP THE pieces of my shattered heart. There were many nights I cried on my pillow in the midnight hour because I missed my husband. It was not easy to adjust to this major change in my life. Yet, I began to seek God with my whole heart and asked Him to show me–me. He showed me the places where I had been in disobedience to His Word.

I continued to go to school despite my broken and bleeding heart. I worked diligently every day to keep up with my studies. Still, I was more focused on the whereabouts of my husband than I was on anything else.

One evening, I went over to his house to bring over some mail. I knocked and when he came to the door he looked as if he had seen a ghost. He immediately asked me to leave. I told him why I was there, but he didn't want to hear it. He told me if I didn't leave, he would call the police on me. I know there was a woman in the house that night, and he was careful to not let me see her.

Defeated, I left.

On my way home, the police stopped me and questioned me about coming to his house. They encouraged me to go home before I was arrested. This was enough for me. He had moved on and didn't want any part of me.

I continued to move forward in school. When it was time for my final exam, I went into class on that morning with hopes of passing and moving on to my nurse's pinning ceremony and graduation.

After talking the exam, our class decided to practice for the pinning ceremony. We all headed to the auditorium while continuously checking the website for our final grade. The grades were being revealed to my classmates one by one. But for some odd reason I couldn't pull my grade up on the website. It was after I arrived to my car that my grade came up. I had failed my nursing class by two points.

I was devastated to learn I had not passed. I fell into a deeper state of depression and despair. I couldn't figure out what was happening to me. It felt like everything in my life was crumbling. I called my husband with hopes of being comforted but ended up feeling he was a little happy over my failing grade. His attitude that day served as a motivator to focus on my job with hopes of being admitted back into nursing school in the fall.

———

JUNE 2014 CAME WITH YET ANOTHER BLOW TO MY HEART. I WAS providing patient care on the day I was told to close out and hand over my computer and leave the premises. This was one of my favorite nursing jobs. I was suspended until after a meeting with administration. I was terminated.

God opens doors because I was employed that same day of my termination by a home health care agency. I was accepted back into nursing school in fall 2014 where I worked hard and passed.

I graduated May 2015 with my Associates Degree in Nursing. God blessed me with a RN job at our local hospital before I passed my nursing boards. After I received my RN license I enrolled and was accepted into a highly recognized university to study for my Bachelor's in Nursing (BSN). This program came with lots of challenges. My children played a major role in my success in obtaining my BSN degree.

---

THERE WERE MANY ISSUES THAT CAME UP AFTER OUR SEPARATION. I could not see the plan of God while in that toxic relationship. I allowed my jealousy, anger, and resentment to block God's plan for my life. I realize the separation was necessary for me to get to the place of surrender unto God.

I realize my God is a jealous God and He does not want nothing placed before Him. I literally made my husband a god and lord of my life. I realize now that God had to remove me from this toxic relationship for me to be the vessel of honor, He has called me to be. My spirit leaped when God told me that when He bless me no one would be able to get the Glory that belongs to Him. I was on the threshing floor before God for years while He dealt with my anger, bitterness, jealousy, and attitude. God has given the joy I've longed for in my life.

My valley experience with losing my husband prepared me for who and where I am today. God had to remove me from that environment to wash me and cleanse me with his Word. He also taught me through His Word how to be a praying wife as He prepares me for my husband.

---

ON DECEMBER 15, 2018, I GRADUATED WITH MY BACHELOR'S IN Nursing. Before graduation day, I was honored to be highlighted on the nurse's page of my school's website. I was also highlighted for the month of February 2019 on a major nurse's association website. I felt like God was giving me "beauty for ashes." I stop fighting and allowed God to lead and guide me. God is doing some amazing things in my life.

In March 2019, I was accepted into the Master's in Nursing (MSN) program. The Graduate Record Examination (GRE) was waived because my GPA meet the admission requirements.

I want to encourage anyone who may read my story. Don't allow your circumstances to dictate your destiny. Continue to seek God for the plan for your life and surrender your entire life to Him. It will not always be easy but make up in your mind to surrender and submit to

His will. Matthew 6:33 (NKJV) says, *but seek first the kingdom of God and His righteousness, and all these things shall be added to you.* God wants us to seek Him with our whole heart. Not for things, but for Him, and everything we need He will add to us. I've found that no one can do me like Jesus. He is a friend that sticks closer than a brother.

God has shown himself mighty and strong in my life. I allowed Him into my heart, and he has shown me great and mighty things. Luke 1:37 says, "*For with God nothing will be impossible.* I'm working diligently to be all I can be for God as my journey continues...

# AUTHOR BIO: CAROLYN HUNTER

Carolyn Hunter is a humble servant of God, a mother of two children, and grandmother. She is a licensed minister and boldly proclaims the Word of God and sings His praises. She continuously declares and decrees Luke 1:37 – "For with God nothing shall be impossible."

Carolyn is a Registered Nurse who works for a Family Medical Practice in North Carolina. She began her nursing career at 45 years of age. With God and determination, she graduated in 2018 from the University of North Carolina – Wilmington (UNCW) with her BSN in nursing.

Before entering the profession of nursing, Carolyn worked in retail management for over 28 years, which helped to develop communication skills used today in her nursing profession. Through trials and tribulations, Carolyn stands strong in God while pursuing her master's in nursing at UNCW.

# TAKING FLYTE

## Kelonyee Sloan

# CHAPTER 1

## Tom, Dick & Harry

"I DON'T WANT SOMEONE EVERY TOM, DICK, AND HARRY HAS HAD their hands on...," He snapped.

"Or C.J. for that matter," I replied. "You haven't touched me in over a month, not even a kiss good night. So why does it even matter who or what has touched me?"

The next thing I knew, I was pinned to the floor of the back seat of my car by 250 lbs. tethered to the knee in my chest. Next came the back to back blows of a closed fist to my face. Thankfully, I was wearing my glasses which buffered the blows and prevented any permanent eye injury. Make-up would conceal the bruising and discoloration that lingered for over a month. However, I didn't own any make-up. I finally appreciated having a daughter, who on most days refused to walk to the mailbox without her beauty enhancements. In my case it was more like war paint. Lark's skilled and gentle hands strategically applied concealer and liquid foundation to mask my battle scars.

I was in a daze as the car seemed to drive itself nonstop for two hours straight to my mother's driveway. Debra Cox's song was on repeat and faintly playing all the way to my Mom's. It kept playing in my head even after the engine had stopped and the CD player silenced.

*How did I get here? I'm not supposed to be here. A victim of domestic violence.* A victim wearing an invisible scarlet letter A after 20 years of marriage to a deacon in the church.

*How did I get here, I'm not supposed to be here sitting in my mother's driveway battered and bruised emotionally and physically? How did I get here? I'm not supposed to be here. Ashamed to look in the mirror. Not solely because of the ugly black eye, but ashamed of the ugly lie I was living.*

The lie was hidden behind my smile and sunny disposition I often portrayed. I was painfully hiding behind a facade each time I walked into my home with my three amazing gifts: Lark, Kaden, and Landon, the fruit of my marital union. I buried that lie Sunday to Sunday as I sat in the church pew. I was able to temporarily transcend above the deception each time I graced the airport concourse to fly coast to coast and global.

I deceived not only myself, but others that I was happily married to the man of my dreams; that he was deeply in love with me. No amount of detox tea could flush our toxins away and restore our hemorrhaging marriage. It was dying on the vine, although we both claimed to be abiding in the True Vine. We were dead men walking in my opinion.

I'd read somewhere that not all storms come to disrupt your life, but to clear your path. I'd seemingly just entered the eye of my storm and wasn't so sure that statement was true. However, I was ready to find out. There was, no place like home for me. I just wished my father was still on this side of life and on the other side of the front door. He could talk me off any ledge even if he was the person who drove me there. Our conversations usually left me feeling like I could face any and every giant that came my way. My father was the wisest man I knew. He always had an answer for everything whether I wanted to hear it or not. Yet, he gave me the freedom to fail and loved me unconditionally which provided a foundation for success.

My parents provided a loving and nurturing home to spread my wings and fly. They were not perfect, but they were a healthy, loving example of conflict resolution void of verbal and physical abuse. They had passionate conversations without abusing boundaries or being disrespectful. My parents are the reason I maintained hope that I could soar despite my marital clipped wings and climate in my home unsweet home. I was determined to rise above the storm and cruise at an altitude that would allow me to soar successfully. I guess that is why I was standing at mom's front the door and ready to knock.

# CHAPTER 2

## No Place Like Home

I KNOCKED ON MOM'S DOOR. A SENSE OF CALM CAME OVER ME AS I heard her footsteps approaching the door. My parent's home has always been a judgement-free zone. I just didn't want to add more disappointment and worry to her plate from the trials of her adult son who was battling his own demons. I was still in my uniform lugging my work and marital baggage from my three-day trip and twenty-year marriage.

She opened the door saying, "What a pleasant..." but stopped mid-sentence when she saw my face. No amount of make-up could hide what was underneath from the most intuitive mom on the planet.

I gave a halfhearted hug and rolled past my mom, leaving the physical baggage in the living room and headed to the kitchen.

I sat at the round table. Mom had followed behind me like a puppy dog without saying a word. She took a seat across from me.

Steve Harvey's voice from Family Feud show playing in the background broke up the silence.

My mind traveled back to the only other time I had seen that look of disappointment on her face. I was a junior in high school. She and my father had caught me in a lie about babysitting. Mom had called to ask a question only to have Mrs. Alston tell her that she hadn't seen me and wasn't in need of my babysitting services that day. Mom's intuition led them exactly to where I was forbidden to go. A boy's house whose parents were home and welcomed my presence. My parents were the ones with reservations, and their rules were that I could receive male company at our supervised home. Except this young man was not allowed to visit. Mom was upset that I had looked her in the eyes and lied to her.

History was repeating itself.

Another selfish act of dishonesty and betrayal minus the verbal and physical abuse backlash. More heartbreak and broken trust that needed to be restored. I had hidden this lie for three months while participating in counseling sessions in an effort to escape the deep dark pit, mend my broken wings while trying to put the broken pieces of broken promises and marriage back together.

"What happened?" Mom asked, her voice calm but filled with tension.

Ironically I heard Steve Harvey say, "Name something a wife hides from her husband."

The contestant blurted out, "Her weight," which was the number one answer for a win. However, the number two answer was an affair —none of the contestants came up with that as an answer.

I looked at my mom and said, "The number two response is what happened. Your daughter had an *affair*."

I watched as my mother's face transformed from shock to disappointment to profound sadness.

I began to share my truth.

# CHAPTER 3

## Truth and Nothing but MY Truth

IT STARTED WHEN WE LOST OUR HOUSE TO FORECLOSURE.

Christopher James, or C.J., suddenly seemed to be a million miles away despite the fact we were cohabitating under the same roof. He'd agreed to move into a house my mother purchased. We would stay there until our credit improved.

The plan was for her to move into the basement he move into the unfinished basement he could magically renovate. I was not upset with him over the loss. This setback was merely a set up for our comeback, I assured him. Our identities were not tied to the size of our home. Our character before, during and after the storm was my measuring stick. I was actually relieved that our rent was less than our mortgage, giving us breathing room to restructure our financial portfolio.

Furthermore, for the first-time our teenage sons would each have their own bedrooms, and I would finally have a basement. Even our dog Chico would have the freedom to roam in the fenced in backyard. My primary concern was keeping the boys in their current school district until high school graduation which was satisfied as well. Kaden was a freshman in high school and Landon was in middle school. Lark had begun her freshman year of college. Everyone was transitioning into very important stages of their lives academically and socially. I wanted to maintain a sense of familiarity despite our personal turmoil.

C.J. was in the process of modifying our home mortgage after the real estate crisis setback. His real estate ventures had slowed tremendously, but his properties were maintaining themselves due to his paying tenants. We had taken the children out of private and home-schooling settings and placed them into reputable public schools. I didn't require a lot of financial upkeep. However, I was a little high maintenance emotionally. I craved quality and quantity of time as well as stimulating and intimate conversations. For a self-employed builder on the rebound financially from foreclosure and a bankruptcy, my expectations were somewhat draining. C.J. and I were ships passing in the night between his tedious work schedule of long hours and late nights and my job as a flight attendant. The bulk of our time as a couple was spent sitting together on our assigned pew Sundays and sometimes on Wednesdays. Our love and fear of God was our marital glue.

We had gone an entire month void of any meaningful conversation or physical relations which was very unusual for us. C.J. wanted weekly physical intimacy even if he was angry with me. A month-long drought was a warning sign that we were terribly out of balance. Although we were sleeping in the same bed, there was an invisible electric fence in the middle, keeping us from crossing over.

I was starving for our cuddling and pillow talk which sparked our close encounter of the physical kind, so I broke the unspoken vow of silence and asked him out on a cheap dinner date to our local Waffle House. He loved a good omelet, so I thought it was the perfect place for us. He would enjoy the food and I would enjoy our time together.

C.J. agreed to meet me without our offspring. I had worn my favorite Victoria Secret lingerie and fragrances to accentuate my favorite sundress—one that usually sparked a rare compliment. To top it off, I had gone to the salon and had my hair done.

I arrived first and awaited his arrival. He was coming from work. I got out the car and he held the door open, then walked behind me.

The waitress told us to seat ourselves.

I chose a booth in the corner.

Disappointment filled me to the core. There was NO mention of how I looked or smelled. No conversation as he concentrated on his cell phone messages. There was no need for a menu. He ordered the same thing every time: scattered and cheese covered hash browns and a chicken omelet with cheese and mushrooms. No onion. Lemonade no ice. I ordered my usual pecan waffle and plain hash browns.

In the absence of our invisible fence, I reached out and touched his hand and inquired about his day. He didn't look up, but eventually answered, "A lot of ripping and running."

He glanced up as the waitress served our orders, then blessed our food as usual.

I attempted to take a bite of my waffle. But when I opened my mouth, a question flew out instead. "Are we okay?"

No reply.

I put my fork down and proceeded to answer my own question. "C.J., we're not all right and haven't been for the past thirty days. Although we have been thrown an emotional and financial whirlwind these past 6 months, we are truly blessed. God has favored us. My father reaching out from the grave with his VA benefits, and mom is our MVP by finding and financing our new home. Minus a few gray hairs everyone is healthy."

He nodded his head and continued to eat.

"I feel as if we are 30,000 miles apart under the same roof. We both know it's been ice cold in the bedroom and our heat system is working in the house. What are we going to do stick and stay or unstick it?"

Still no answer.

His silence felt like a sledgehammer to my heart.

C.J. finished his food and without looking at me, he said," Unstick it."

"What does that mean?" I asked.

More silence.

I packed my meal in a to-go container and drove home alone where the cold war continued.

# CHAPTER 4

## Too Proud to Beg

I AWOKE THE NEXT MORNING TO MY OWN SELF-TALK.

I AM too proud to beg.

Not that I thought too highly of myself, but because I thought highly of myself.

I AM confident.

I have never begged anyone to like or to love me. I was raised to be self-confident. I was well aware of my worth. My father and mother placed zero limits on what I could do. Before my father had transitioned to the other side of eternity, I reassured him that I would manage my emotions and keep my hands to myself. My last physically disruptive angry outburst was after another bout of the silent treatment that typically was no longer than a week. Usually, C.J.'s silence was a preventive measure that was out of balance. He wanted to keep the peace and to avoid behavior he would later regret or could not retract. I remembered one of our marital classes at church our counselors sharing that we had to go through conflict before getting to our desired intimacy. We could not sweep things under the rug that needed to be addressed nor should we ignore our elephant in the room.

C.J. felt the classes were a waste of time. I needed to learn when to be quiet and to submit to my husband in all things. I had learned to embrace our conflict in hopes of getting to a place of intimacy. That might look like throwing things, unplugging the television, or spraying him with a water bottle to stir up the necessary conflict in order to enter a period of intimacy.

Wasn't a good woman worth a good fight? If only the fighting didn't escalate to dangerous exchanges of words which would then lead to battle scars. Our last battle Royale before we lost the house was a head banger. I locked myself in my car and called my father to talk us both off the cliff. That was the night I made the promise that I would not continue in this abusive manner.

The morning after the Waffle House dinner date, I got dressed for work without any deviations from my usual routine. I said good-bye to C.J. and informed him I was scheduled to return Thursday afternoon.

I didn't wait around for a response. I still despised the silent treatment and was bracing for landing from whatever his "unstick it" comment pertained to since he refused to clarify.

I was starving for a hug and a kiss before getting back up in the air. I believed in leaving on a positive note since tomorrow isn't promised. My good-bye was all the positive I could muster from within me considering the present wind chill factor in the bedroom. I had no problem agreeing to disagree or loving unconditionally when the behavior may have been unlovely. How many times had I heard or taught my children in bible class that love suffers long and is kind? Even better, the lesson that Christ loved and died for us while we were yet a sinner.

C.J. was an advocate of the saying that love speaks louder than any words. With that being the case, I wasn't feeling the love he professed 20 years ago on our wedding day.

# CHAPTER 5

## The Layover

IT WAS ANOTHER TYPICAL LONG DUTY DAY OF UP AND DOWN LONG flights, upset passengers, and crying kids, the fifteen-hour layover in Austin, Texas. As I was passing out hotel room keys to my crew members, a familiar voice called my name, I turned to find a friendly face for my tired and sore eyes.

One of my favorite homeboys, Tony Jernigan was standing in front of me to my surprise. We exchanged hugs. He told me he was there on business and was taking a break from a long boring meeting. He asked me to accompany him for dinner. My crew and I were to leave tomorrow afternoon and since I normally didn't eat dinner after six p.m.—it was too late for dinner. He insisted that I grab an appetizer with him or at the very least join him for a late drink.

I pondered the idea of accepting his invitation. I hadn't seen Tony in two years. He had been a great friend in high school. I decided to join him and we headed downstairs to the hotel's restaurant.

After studying the menu, I found nothing I wanted to eat. I was trying to watch my calories and this selection wasn't helping, I eventually decided on a side salad with vinaigrette, after which I excused myself to the restroom. When I returned, I found that he'd ordered me a glass of wine.

Tony wasn't aware that I'd stopped drinking since CJ didn't drink alcohol. Nevertheless, I took a sip, then another and another. I never subscribed to my husband's philosophy that drinking was a sinful act— I believed one could drink sociably if they could maintain self-control.

Tony was divorced and appeared to be adjusting well to the single life. However, he did mention he was looking forward to finding another wife. We spent the evening talking about the usual stuff; our kids, our jobs, and mutual friends. At some point, the conversation turned to specifics about my marriage. Tony teased me about how my blind date turned into a shotgun wedding which lasted twenty years when most high-school sweetheart unions failed long before the seven-year itch.

I laughed. My father never pulled out his shotgun at all. Despite the fact my mother knew I was pregnant, C.J. had charmed both my parents. Although, we had only known one another for a month, he assured my father that he had every intention of marrying me and taking care of his unborn child.

I was unsure of the marriage thing. It was so permanent. I didn't think we knew one another well enough to talk about marriage. C.J. was in the process of buying his first home, and he wanted to fill it with more than furniture. He was ready to get married.

All my mother wanted was for me to get married while my dad was like, "Move in with him until you figure it out. You and this child are his responsibility."

———

FOR THE NEXT FEW WEEKS I WAS ON A JOURNEY TO FIND PEACE WITH God and find an answer for my dilemma. I knew that none of my girl-friends would ever advise me to get married due to a baby. There was a fleeting thought of terminating the pregnancy. When I mentioned this to C.J., he was adamantly opposed to the idea but left the decision up to me. He told me he would pay for it. However, he warned that if I went through with it—this would adversely affect our relationship. Adoption was also an option which led to a heated discussion about who would keep the baby, which yielded more issues.

I struggled with the idea of not having a year to get to know him for all four seasons prior to our nuptials. I wanted to experience C.J.'s changing moods through each season, I wanted to know more about him but there was no time. Four months after my blind date I agreed to marry for better or worse.

Reliving my past with C.J., I burst into tears at the thought of losing everything, including my marriage. It was all too much.

Tony gave me a shoulder to cry on and a tissue to wipe my tears. He shifted his seat to get into the booth beside me and rubbed my back to settle my cries.

# CHAPTER 6

## The Betrayal

A QUIET STORM WAS BREWING.

Tony escorted me to my room. There had been no sexual innuendos exchanged the entire evening. I was perfectly sober—I never finished that one glass of wine, but I felt tipsy from that soul baring conversation. Tony's obvious concern, kind words and consoling embrace was intoxicating. I had been deprived of adult conversation between a man and a woman for months.

Tony graciously turned on all the lights in my hotel room and declared, "The coast is clear no Boogeyman in here."

He extended his arms to give me a hug good night but for some reason I couldn't let go—his well-intentioned actions ignited an awakening of passion, I hadn't felt in a long time.

In this moment, I was about to betray my husband.

# CHAPTER 7

## Self-Help

I'M SURE C.J. NEVER ONCE IMAGINED THAT I WOULD BE THE ONE TO turn our marriage upside down and break his heart. That I would be the one to violate the marriage bed.

After three months of counseling, I learned how to express my real emotions without fear of judgement. The salt of my tears burned but as time went by my remorse turned into relief. I was relieved with the realization that I was not void of passion. Somehow, I had become comfortably numb to the touch of my husband. It was as if the one thing that would destroy my marriage, would also be the thing that caused my rebirth. C.J. and I were broken long before that night. My affair was merely a result of our brokenness. After the physical violence, my therapist could not ethically counsel C.J. and I together.

I was determined to fly once I recovered from my personal injuries. Hopefully, C.J. would choose to do the same. I wanted us to fly together at the same altitude but only time would bear witness of this. He agreed to working on our friendship if we could be friends with benefits.

# CHAPTER 8

## Same Page

AFTER A MONTH OF SEPARATE THERAPY SESSIONS C.J. FELT LIKE WE were on the road to recovery and no longer needed the third parties. We had seemingly gotten onto the same page.

One evening, C.J. decided to open up. He said, "I honestly appreciate everything that you and your mother did to help our family stay afloat after losing our home. I just felt that you were excluding me. As the man of the house I wasn't even able to participate in my own family's rescue. I didn't mean to take it out on you with the silence. I was grieving the loss of what we had worked so hard to maintain. It was almost 20 years we'd had that house. I just don't understand how you could kick a man while he's down by violating our marriage vows. I have never touched a woman since I said I do to you. I would die for you and our family.

There's no man alive who can replace the values I represent and fight for. I agree that I left you vulnerable during my silence. However, it was never an excuse for you to do what you did. I haven't even seen you shed a tear. It was as if you had no remorse and no humility and no concern about how you were destroying our marriage and family. I am beyond hurt. I don't understand why you couldn't love me enough after all we've been through."

I interrupted C.J., "You're wrong. I cried every day when I was on my trips. I've been suffering in silence bracing myself for what may come. My counselor has been helping me put out the flames from our crash and burn of a marriage during these months of separate counseling. I'm actually on the stretcher being carried to the ambulance so to speak. You on the other hand, are still inside the burning aircraft you are crawling trying to get to an open exit. You survived the crash but the question you must answer is will you fly again after your burn wounds are treated and healed? I appreciate your transparency, patience, and willingness to forgive and attempts to fly again with me."

# CHAPTER 9

## Clear Air Turbulence

THREE YEARS PASSED WITH US CRUISING ALONG WITH JUST AN occasional light chop or conflict. No battle scars No severe turbulence. We had seemingly fallen back into our usual routine of family, church and work. I had decided to recommit to a new health and wellness team. Which turned out to be the beginning of the end. A girlfriend had challenged me to lose five lbs. in five days by drinking and organic detox tea. I watched her drink and shrink and didn't want to be left behind.

My initial five lb. loss turned into an eventual 35 lb. loss of unwanted waste and weight. While I was physically detoxing with the tea and other wellness supplements, my marriage was becoming increasingly more toxic. The person whom I wanted to be my biggest fan, was my worst critic. He occasionally commented that he wasn't worried about my weight. He couldn't seem to understand that I needed to take back my body, so that I'd be able to live a long and healthy life.

During Kaden's senior year of high school, I contracted pneumonia and ended up in the hospital for a week and out of work for 2 months. CJ was most content whenever I needed him to provide for me. What nobody knew was that prior to my illness, we'd had an argument and

CJ had threatened to leave once again. My illness was a smoke screen and just a temporary delay to his final departure.

One day after taking Kaden to college, CJ announced that he was unhappy and if I didn't make some changes, he had no choice but to leave. I agreed and suggested that we go back to counseling. He agreed but it never materialized.

When he finally decided to move out, he thought maybe his absence would make me appreciate his presence.

# CHAPTER 10

## Taking Flight

THIS WAS THE FINAL EXODUS.

I was hurt and disappointed C.J. didn't want to fight for our marriage. I wasn't too proud to beg him to stay. I simply refused to do so.

The reality of what was really going on in my life opened my eyes. I had been so busy loving everyone else that I'd neglected to love myself more. I had forgotten to place my own oxygen mask on myself first before helping others. The affair that once weighed heavily on me —no longer held that kind of power. I am not afraid to fly after crashing under the weight of my infidelity. It was a valuable lesson during life's flight school. Another lesson I had to learn was to forgive myself.

I continue to fly. There is nothing left to do except to fly higher with the wind of my faith, family and friends beneath my wings. My flight cabin is ready for take-off. Bright skies and great weather ahead. But even in the midst of the storms which sometimes come, I will continue to soar.

# AUTHOR BIO: KELONYEE SLOAN

For the past 28 years I have been working for a major airline, maintaining a marriage and raising children on the fly. After 26 years, the marriage crashed and burned from the residue of toxic communication, financial fall out ,and broken vows.

Today, I am no longer grounded from oversized baggage. I have new lightweight carry-on bags which can only hold my personal items. My hands are free, so I can place my oxygen mask on MYSELF frst before helping others.

My wings have always existed. All I have to do is FLY. I am grateful for my family and friends who are the winds beneath my wings. I Am beyond ready to take flight to my divinely designed destination.

# BORN

## Charniece Harris

# CHAPTER 1

## What's the Point?

IF THE ENEMY HAD HIS WAY, I WOULD BE DOA (DEAD ON ARRIVAL). But God! My mother was only 17 years old when she became pregnant with me. Back then, it was not as acceptable as it is now—my grandmother was embarrassed. Appearance meant everything to her, so she attempted home remedies hoping to cause my mother to miscarry. My mother, determined to keep her baby, ran away from home to Kansas City where I was born. My mom never graduated from high school because of her decision to keep me. I always felt guilty for being born. I used to wonder if my arrival in this world created any love, joy, or happiness for anyone. It seemed as if all the people in my life had one regret or another for my existence.

Due to my mother's inability to care for me, I ended up being raised by her mom; and my grandmother reminded me often of the struggle to take care of me in addition to her own children. She worked a full-time job and part-time as a cook for a white family. My grandmother was very strict. She yelled and cursed all the time and didn't hesitate to beat your butt with whatever was convenient. Some of my beatings were warranted, but some were just cruel and unusual punishment. I used to joke that until I was 15 years old, I thought my name was motherf**king b**.

She always said I was going to be just like my mother. My grand-mother seemed angry and sad all the time. Expressions of affection such as hugs and kisses were nonexistent. The clothes on your back and food on the table were my indicators of love, except the birthday cards that were always signed:

*Pray...*
*Love, Mother*

I know I was a constant reminder of my mom, who my grand-mother said was the only child she wanted and the one she wished she'd never had. My grandfather was a quiet man who left the house early and came home late, oftentimes catching the brunt of his wife's anger.

On Sundays, we watched football, Wild Kingdom and 60 Minutes together. I don't know exactly how he felt about me being there—it didn't seem to affect him one way or the other. This was not the case with my Aunt Bethe. She was the youngest of my mother's siblings and only 4 years separated us. She made no secret of her disdain for me. On many occasions, she mistreated me. Ultimately, I had to beat her behind one good time to get her to stop the physical abuse. There was also Aunt Sue, who being eight years older than me, seemed more like a mother figure.

Most people aspire to be like their parents. I was torn. My mom was well known for several reasons. On one hand, she was described as the smartest and most beautiful girl in school. In that aspect, I wanted to be like her. On the other hand, she was described as a class-less, home wrecking drug addict. I vowed no one would ever say those things about me. Little did I know that I would end up repeating some of that same behavior; that I would fight some of the same demons. I had no idea that there would be times when I'd wish I had never been born.

My relationship with my mother has always been complicated; riddled with moments and seasons of resentment and gratitude, joy and pain, laughter and crying, love and sometimes hate. Her presence was sporadic, which led to me referring to her as my holiday/birthday mom.

At one point, we were more like sisters. One day she caught me smoking a cigarette and told me then that whatever I thought I was grown enough to do—I could do in front of her. This proved to be a pivotal point in our relationship; one that I would grow to regret.

In the beginning, I was glad to have a cool mom. My friends and I hung out at her house drinking, smoking cigarettes, and making out. This coolness gave birth to the ability to be disrespectful to her and my disrespect gave my friends the permission to be that way. However, this didn't sit well with me.

Over the years, I began to long for a regular mother. Then there was the role reversal. Her childlike, irresponsible ways often made me forget who the parent was, and for a while I became the mother. I would be the one to rescue her from bad situations. I was the one who provided a place for her to stay on more than one occasion to help get her back on her feet. I was the one sending money every month to the babysitter to help with expenses for my little brother. I was the one who defended her when people talked trash about her. She was mine and I loved her.

Daddy is another story altogether. He was a Marine. He was away in Vietnam when I was born. He saw me for the very first time on my first birthday. They tell me that up until that point I only crawled but when I saw him, I took off running. I guess there is nothing like the love of a daughter for her father. Unfortunately, I would not get to experience the depth of that love due to his being absent most of my life along with his family.

I was 42 years old before I saw them again. I went to Kansas City with high expectations of a grand reunion, but there was no red carpet for me. By the time it was over, I left feeling more damaged than I did prior to going. He wanted me to be his baby girl and although part of me longed to be just that, another facet wanted him to know that I was a grown woman who had fared well without him. Truth of the matter is that I had no real idea how much my father's absence had affected and shaped my life. Being in his presence magnified all the hurt and pain I'd suppressed over the years.

We bumped heads constantly, fighting to express our feelings while trying to make the other understand. I wanted to know why didn't he come for me, send for me, provide for me, or love me? At best, I got a phone call every 2-3 years filled with broken promises. He owed me, or so I thought. He was unapologetic and felt that I needed to just get over it. It was a rude awakening and valuable lesson I learned on that trip. I promised myself I would never go back. I thanked God for allowing me to meet my grandmother; got my bags and with a made-up mind, defiant spirit, and a cold heart. He was dead to me and I meant it. I told myself that I didn't need him anyway. He hadn't done anything for me. My anger lasted for quite some time and the pain lasted longer.

Loving, respecting, and honoring my parents had never been an easy task for me to accomplish. I felt justified in holding grudges, being bitter, and wallowing in self-pity. They were responsible for bringing me here. Even as an adult, I blamed them for all the wrong in my life. I was able to deflect my bad behavior from scrutiny by constantly reminding others of the bad hand I had been dealt. I was able to play on people's sympathy for many years. I held guilt and shame over my mother's head like an umbrella. I constantly reminded her of the mistakes she made, how she wasn't there, etc....I never let her forget. I wreaked havoc for many years, lashing out simply because I was hurting.

# CHAPTER 2

## Masks

TO SOMEONE ON THE OUTSIDE LOOKING IN, I APPEARED TO BE A normal kid. I was able to blend with my surroundings. I did and said whatever necessary to be accepted. I mastered this skill. I managed to be productive in school; I've been promoted on just about every job ever held, and sustained meaningful, long-term relationships with the opposite sex. I accomplished this without having any identity of self. I suffered in silence well into my adult life. It played such a huge part in who I would become and the roads I would travel. I was amazed at how I was able to fool people. If they looked a little more closely though, they would've been able to see the cracks in my disguise, evidenced by my acts of rebellion, defiance, and aggression.

I learned early that a woman could use her body to get whatever she wanted from a man. However, I was far from a woman when the violations took place. At the tender age of five, I was molested by my next-door neighbor. I had no idea that's what it was called. I just know that if I touched him between his legs and allowed him to touch me, I could hang with him in the shed and play with his bike. He seemed to really like me, and I enjoyed being liked. It would not be the last time that emotional starvation would cause me to do things that were not proper. At that age, however, I had no clue about that.

When I was in the third grade, a friend of mine had an older cousin who offered us twenty-five cents to allow him to touch our bodies. Thankfully, someone came home before anything could take place and I was spared that time. I thought it strange that my friend was so willing, but I figured there really wasn't anything wrong with it. When I saw her cousin on a different day, he offered to walk me home from the recreational center. I accepted his offer without hesitation. He took me on a shortcut that consisted of a path along the side of an ditch where he offered me money and began fondling me. I didn't like the feeling, especially when he tried to kiss me. After a couple of minutes, he tried to put his hand in my pants. The more I struggled—the more persistent he became. We were interrupted when a neighborhood friend appeared. He stopped and grabbed my hand and squeezed it as if to say, "Be quiet."

I took off running. When I arrived home, I told my Aunt Beth what happened. She seemed upset and proceeded to tell my grandmother. A couple of days later, his aunt came to the house and I was questioned about the incident. I don't know what was said between the two women, but it was swept under the rug. That decision taught me to keep my mouth shut because my word didn't matter. My friend was upset with me and told people I tried to get her cousin in trouble. She denied that he offered us money to touch our bodies. I was hurt and felt betrayed.

A few years later, that same guy was imprisoned for raping a 5-year-old girl. I felt vindicated. I had the opportunity to see him again years later. So many emotions rushed in like a flood. He dropped his head, wanting to avoid eye contact. I wasn't going to let him off that easy. I made sure everyone in the store knew he was a sexual predator. I will never forget the look on his face. One of guilt and shame, pleading for mercy.

I didn't care. I hurled insults and made obscene gestures. I never considered whether God had delivered him while he was in prison—it didn't matter. He had hurt me. His expression of shame and pleading for mercy would become all too familiar in my own life. One I would wear time and time again.

Growing up, there was one violation after another. Some I allowed for monetary gain like the old man who lived around the corner from my house. Actually, I could get to his house through a path from my back yard. Every Friday, I would go there and allow him to grope my breast for a few dollars. He always told me how beautiful I was. In a way, he filled the void in my life; my pocket and my need for positive affirmation. Then there was the man who owned a couple of boarding houses in the neighborhood. He knew my mom and treated me nice. He had plenty of money and lots of liquor at his place. He would take me to get fast food, put money in my pocket and allow me to drink all I wanted. This, of course, came at a price. He used his fingers to penetrate me and would kiss my breasts. This behavior ceased at the age of 14 when I got my first real boyfriend. His name was Phil and he was five years older than me.

He was the first person with whom I had real sexual intercourse. He became my world, consuming my thoughts and time. He dictated where I went, who I talked to, what I wore; basically, my entire being. He was a tough guy. Some folks said he murdered a white lady. He was also my abuser mentally, emotionally, and ultimately physically. I was raped three times during my tenure in this relationship; once by a stranger, once by a classmate of Aunt Beth, and once by Phil himself. Humiliation was not the word I associated with my feelings at the time, but it is the right description looking back. When When my aunt's classmate raped me, I told my boyfriend. He spoke with the guy who told him I consented. There were some angry words exchanged between them, but I did not get the results I was hoping for—Phil no longer trusted me.

I was the victim.

The story leaked out into the streets and that guy dragged my name through the mud. It was a difficult time and I regretted ever opening my mouth. Again, my words meant nothing. I became the master of suppression. I had no clue how badly this would affect my ability or inability to cope, express myself, or have honest relationships.

I was on my way to Phil's house when the second rape occurred. I'd made the mistake of catching a ride with this stranger. Thankfully, I survived and made it to Phil's an hour later than anticipated.

As soon as Phil opened the door, I apologized profusely and told him that I'd stopped by a friend's house to get him a surprise and it had taken more time than I planned. I wasn't going to make the mistake of mentioning the rape. I presented him with the two joints, which seemed to placate him. I told him that the walk had me sweaty and wanted to take a quick shower. The water streaming down, hid the tears I shed.

My secret was safe. A deceiver was born.

Phil shaped and molded my definition of love as it pertained to the opposite sex. He was tall, dark-skinned, a great dresser and smooth talker. My grandmother despised him. She felt that he was too old and experienced for me. The more she tried to tear us apart—the more determined we were to stay together. There was no stopping me. Many times, I ran away to spend the night at his house. All of my spare time was spent with him. He was my transportation back and forth to school on many days.

Phil was a severe womanizer and I found myself on the other end of conflict and pain more often than I care to remember. He was a pro at manipulation and intimidation. Part of me was afraid to leave and the other part just didn't want to in spite of the pain. When I found out he was cheating again, I took the opportunity to break it off. I tried to start a new relationship. However, this was short-lived. Phil's threats scared off anyone else who may have had interest in me.

I eventually went back to him. For a while, things seemed to get better. Then one day it was as if a light bulb went off. I was done. I found the courage to tell him it was over and meant it. He stalked me everywhere I went. He broke into my grandmother's house on three separate occasions. He even persuaded my mother to plot with him to get me alone, then raped me inside her home. She had given him a key. I could never understand how my own mother could place me in this position? This incident changed the course of my already-strained relationship with my mom.

I became cold-hearted and manipulative. I'd learned from some of the best. I took those lessons and flipped the script. I used sex and played mind games to get what I wanted. I was the one in charge. A selfish, manipulative abuser was born.

# CHAPTER 3

## Makings of a Rock Star

AT AGE EIGHT I TOOK MY FIRST DRINK, AND I SMOKED MY FIRST JOINT eleven. I experimented with pills in junior high school, but it wasn't my cup of tea. One friend tried to show me how to sniff cocaine, but I didn't catch on at that time. Unfortunately, I would get another chance after graduation. I attended college at Winston Salem State University. This was my Aunt Sue'a alma mater. When I ran into a homeboy, who was a classmate of Sue, but had not yet graduated, my attendance really took a nosedive. He had his own apartment and it was a party all the time. I graduated from smoking reefer to sniffing cocaine and free basing. I barely made it through the first semester.

When we returned from Christmas break that year, I never made it back to campus. I had my ride to drop me off at my homeboy's and what happened next is what horror movies are made from. His house was the Zoo. There was a mixture of all walks of life; street walkers, dope fiends, prostitutes, college kids, locals, foreigners, drug dealers, business professionals, black, white and brown. You name it. Getting high was the primary goal each day for everyone that crossed his threshold.

At the Zoo, there were orgies and females degraded themselves to get more drugs. Even though I was there, I was never forced to participate in the lewd activities, maybe because he knew my family. I was often told that I stood out like a sore thumb and didn't belong there. They called me college girl.

I had a boyfriend at the time who was in school. He would come by to visit and plead with me to come back to school. I always resented him being there because I couldn't participate in the get high activities going on in the back. We would sit out front and drink. Sometimes we had sex and then I would persuade him to leave with the promise that I would come to campus tomorrow.

I finally broke down and told him what I had really been doing. I know he was already suspicious and people on campus had started to spread rumors about me. I didn't care if he left me, I just wanted to get high. Surprisingly, he said he wanted to try it. That was the beginning of the end of our relationship. After that all he wanted to do was get high whenever he came over. He no longer encouraged me to go back to campus. Eventually I returned to Kinston.

The friend who'd initially tried to show me how to snort cocaine, told me that they were using something called "ready rock." I had no clue what I was getting ready to embark on when I took that first pull. It would be another month before I saw my family and I was in the same city. I had worried my grandmother almost to death. She was happy and angry at same time when I finally showed up.

I escaped death time and time again, putting myself in situations that could have ended badly. But for the grace... After a stay in Goldsboro, NC, Hyattsville, Maryland, another in Winston Salem, NC, and Raleigh, NC, I finally ended up in Charlotte, NC and my life gained some stability. I moved there to be close to my best friend. Soon after my arrival, my roommates and I got evicted. Homeless, we moved into a motel in downtown Charlotte.

Initially, only one of us had employment so times were hard. We barely had food to eat and, on some nights, we went to bed hungry. Eventually, we all found jobs. We didn't have transportation, but thankfully our jobs were downtown Charlotte as well. After being told we had to leave our initial motel due to a conference and the room was needed, we ended up living in another one known as a place for swingers and all other types of sexual activity.

The managers made it clear to everyone that we were not to be bothered or approached for sex. We didn't want to be there, but it was all we could afford. I turned 21 in that motel. We learned to make the best of things and prayed for an apartment.

I met a guy named John on my job who was nice enough to allow us to stay with him until we could get one. We called ourselves "John's angels."

This lasted three months.

Six months after the initial eviction, we were in our own apartment. Life was good. During this time, I continued to drink but avoided drugs. That is, until I met this girl from New York who worked on my job. She and her boyfriend relocated to NC after an attempt on his life. He was a drug dealer. We did a lot of cocaine. Eventually, I ran into a homeboy from Kinston, who introduced me to one of his partners from New York. We had a lot of sex and sniffed a lot of cocaine. I became pregnant and lost my job due to my attitude. Life got real instantly.

My first instinct was to abort. What was I going to do with a baby? I informed the guy in Charlotte and he agreed to pay. Once I was on the table, I was informed that they wouldn't be able to perform the procedure. I was 15 and a half weeks pregnant and they didn't go beyond 15 weeks. Jobless, with two possible baby fathers, I moved back to Kinston.

My pregnancy was a lonely one. I had no baby shower. My son was born on 3/22/91 at 11:51 am. He was 7 ½ pounds and 21 inches long. His potential daddy came around after about two weeks. He was skeptical and so was I. Honestly, he favored the guy in Charlotte to me. Then his Aunt saw the baby and told him to stop denying his child. He took ownership after that, but never gave me monetary support. I was good. All I needed was my sweet baby. I often watched him sleep, waiting anxiously for him to wake. He hardly ever cried, and everyone wanted to keep him.

One night, my son fell ill and couldn't keep anything down. I took him to the emergency room. They said he had a stomach virus, to just give him fluids, and if he did not get better in a couple of days to take him to the pediatrician. For the next couple of days, I followed the instructions. He appeared to get better.

The 4th of July was coming and EU, a band from Washington, DC, was going to be at the club. We had been planning for this for quite some time and I had purchased an outfit for the occasion. I had to go. My usual sitters were both going to the club, so I was going to be stuck home. Then one of my friend's mother, offered to keep him. She stayed on the outskirts of Kinston. I was desperate so I agreed. I had a great time that night. I danced all night and afterwards went to a couple of spots trying to see this guy I was interested in. It got late and I did something I never do; I let my son spend the night, but first thing the next morning—I caught a cab to pick up my baby.

When I got there, he didn't look too good. She said he was sick all night, but she didn't know how to contact me. I took him straight to the hospital. We spent hours in the ER. He was shaking and I assumed it was due to being cold. I found out later that he'd had a seizure. He was severely dehydrated. The initial tube was put in wrong and his hand was swollen up like a football. They had to do it again. It was difficult to find a vein and I could tell it was painful. He looked at me with what seemed like despair, but he couldn't cry because he didn't have any tear ducts. It broke my heart.

Eventually the pediatrician arrived and instructed them to admit him immediately. It was three p.m. We had been there since 7:30 that morning.

Everything was going to be all right, so I thought. As soon as we got in his room, the phone rang. It was my grandmother. She had been frantically searching for us. I should have known that she was worried because we never came home the night before, but it never crossed my mind to contact her. I explained the situation and told her she could wait until the next day to come when my Uncle's wife could drive her. We hung up when a nurse entered the room. She told me that he was not out of danger yet. She then asked if I could go to the desk and get another nurse. As soon as I stepped out of the room, Code Blue was called.

To my dismay, they rushed into my son's room. I tried to enter but was blocked from going inside. I called my grandmother from the room next door and told her I needed her to come as soon as she could get there.

My son was placed in ICU. Two major hospitals were contacted for help. It took a total of five hours for them to say they had no bed for him. Then Pitt Memorial was contacted in Greenville, NC. They had a bed available and could take him right then. By this time, his father and my grandmother had arrived. My son was flown to Greenville while we drove—we were only thirty minutes away.

They admitted him and placed me in the Ronald McDonald house. My best friend came from Charlotte to stay with me. My baby had tubes running from every part of his body. As the days went by, there was no improvement. When nothing more could be done, I was given the option to stay or leave when they decided to pull the plug. He was brain dead.

Brokenhearted, I left.

He died July 9, 1991. He wasn't quite 4 months old. I cried a year later while wishing I'd never been born.

# CHAPTER 4

## Bondage No Bars

Life after that was cold.

I went through the motions of living. I appeared to be a strong woman dealing with the loss of her child. I was anything but—in fact, I had no coping skills at all, so I resorted to what I knew best... getting high. I used his death to gain sympathy and for a while the streets treated me good, supplying my every need as it related to drugs.

I moved back to Charlotte several months later once I received the insurance payout. I got an apartment, a job and a new boyfriend. Life appeared normal. We fell into a routine which included drinking on a daily basis. I went through a couple of apartments and a few boyfriends.

———

Three years later, I ran into an old love and we stated dating. It was summer of 1993. For the first two and a half years we commuted and then we decided that I would move to Greensboro. I had an engagement ring, a new job, a new apartment, good friends, and a dog named Brandy.

Life was grand.

We started talking about a date for marriage. We paid for the honeymoon and then I changed my mind. I told Gray that I wanted to buy a home by the age of 30, so I convinced him that postponing the wedding was the right thing to do.

We bought our home in September 1998. I found a duffle bag containing crack cocaine in my home the next month. I resisted temptation at that time because I didn't want to jeopardize my job. I never told my fiancé that I saw it. I figured out the bag belonged to his cousin.

That next month, his cousin came again with the same duffle bag. I didn't resist this time. There was no need. My job had ended. My fiancé worked third shift and his cousin couldn't stay in the house while he was working. I stayed up for 3 full days getting high and no one had a clue. I thought I was going to die. I remember calling my mom asking for help. Her response was, "Can you get some more?"

I was shocked and hurt. I was trying to stop. She was my mother— we never got high together Next, I called my best friend. She told me to pack a bag and come to where she was immediately. I took that option and took Brandy with me. I slept for two days, waking up long enough to eat and use the bathroom. Poor Brandy did the same. She was tired trying to keep up with me.

My fiancé and I had it out when I returned home. I knew he was dealing marijuana, but not cocaine. He was angry when I told him about the drug use. I told him never to bring it in my home again. He made me promise never to use again. We agreed but, in the end, we were both lying. I found more drugs in the house and I used them. He lost his job in March 1999 and things really took a turn for the worse. He was determined never to work for the white man again, so his drug dealing increased. He had tried different legal ventures, but nothing really paid the bills so hustling became his main source of income.

I eventually found another job and settled into the role of being a baller's lady. Our house was the pit stop for everyone and we always had company. I hung out with my girls on the weekend and cooked dinner every Sunday for all of my homies. My mom moved in with us.

After a few months, she went missing for almost thirty days. After flyers were posted in several neighborhoods and a televised plea on the news she resurfaced. She was in a mental institution and had been there after expressing thoughts of suicide to the authorities.

My mother had been hanging with friends using drugs and when she attempted to make her way home, she was raped. According to her, she fell into a depression caused by guilt, shame, humiliation, and fear of letting me know what happened. Somehow, she felt it better to be committed than return home and face me. Somehow, she felt I would be angry and ashamed of her. Truth is, I was petrified. I thought she was dead. I was overjoyed that she wasn't. The anger came later.

The downward spiral called my life was slow but progressive. My using became more frequent, and jobs became harder to keep. The stealing began to cause serious dissension in the home. The lies and infidelities ripped our foundation to pieces. Eventually, the home was lost. Brandy died and in 2003, my fiancé was murdered. He and I had never really parted—we just weren't living together at the time.

I remember the knock on the door, the look on my friend's face letting me know something was terribly wrong; the ride to Greensboro, the acts to alter my mind; the last minute decision to make the funeral after days in a drunken/high stupor; the trip to the mall to get something presentable to wear at my uncle's expense; the overwhelming feeling of rejection of not being allowed to sit with family, the closed casket, the ride to cemetery; the outburst at the sight of the unkept place he would be buried; the engagement ring being placed in the casket, and finally no reason to believe anyone was ever coming to rescue me from me.

———

IN SEPTEMBER 2004, MY GRANDMOTHER BECAME ILL AND WAS UNABLE to live alone. I volunteered to move back to Kinston and help aid in her care. No husband, no children, no real job at the time, and in debt to the drug man. She needed me, but the reality is, I needed her more. Things started out good. They always do. Having to puree my grandmother's food, helping her bathe, and get dressed was something I was not prepared for. Not because it was hard but because it was difficult to see her in this state. It wasn't long before I was using again and because I could not leave her alone for long, I began to get high in the home. I was getting unemployment benefits, but it proved not enough to pay for my car and my drug use. I had to get a job.

Eventually, my mom moved home to help. She arrived in full take over mode. One day when she caught me smoking drugs in the bath-room, she became angry. She asked me if I was crazy and told me I could never use in the house again. That would change when her old bugaboos caught up to her. She came home one night from gambling and told me to go get us one.

It was late at night, but I didn't hesitate to take the money. We had already crossed the lines in Greensboro and started getting high together. This was the beginning of a very dark time in my life and my relationship with my mother. The lines again became blurred and the respect level was at an all-time low. Things came to a head when I asked my mother to loan me some money to pay a drug dealer to get my vehicle back. I was expecting another last check from another lost job. My mother agreed. She told me it was money for the light bill, and I had better pay it back as soon as my check arrived.

That was the plan until I arrived home the next day to overhear her talking about me to one of her friends. She was planning to put me out after I paid her. The check had arrived. I took it off the table and left. I spent it all.

I was banned from the house. I complied under the pretense that I didn't want to bring drama which might upset my grandmother. I was homeless, my vehicle was repossessed. I found a job; I lost a job. When I wasn't getting high, I slept all day and hung out at night. The signs of my abusing drugs were becoming evident.

I moved to Greenville, NC.

# CHAPTER 5

## Breath of Life

IN 2006, THE ZOE HOUSE SAVED MY LIFE. IT WAS A FAITH-BASED HOME for women and children struggling with homelessness, addiction, reintegrating back into society after incarceration, etc. I met the owner when I was employed at the Food Bank previously and lived there for about 10 days, the previous year. That stay ended abruptly when I went to Kinston for a day and never returned due to using. I was told that I would be welcomed back. I decided to take them up on the offer.

It was during this time that I really began to form an intimate relationship with God. We had structured living which was something I needed in my life. I was employed at the community shelter and Hardees, which was very humbling. We had church in the sanctuary at the house and eventually we started a storefront in which I was a very instrumental part of constructing.

---

AFTER A YEAR AND THREE MONTHS, I MOVED OUT OF THE ZOE HOUSE. I was a board member for the home and a full-time, active member of the church. In 2007, I got a job as a correctional officer and began to pursue my degree in Criminal Justice. In 2010, I purchased a new car and a new home. I did not use drugs/alcohol for three and a half years.

Then one day, I decided I wanted a glass of wine with my bath. I began to go back around my old stomping grounds and although it took some time, I was reunited with my old friend, cocaine. I began to miss time from work, and I began to juggle my bill money.

Once again I was in bondage.

I was brutally attacked in my home October 2011 by a man I picked up on the street while looking for drugs. I was arrested for a DUI the following November after leaving my 30th Class Reunion. My license was taken for 30 days. During this time, I was in and out of the hospital, primarily for mental health issues. I abused alcohol, drugs and people when allowed. It all came to a head in February 2012.

The headline on the television stated, "Whitney Houston dead at age 48." I immediately felt a heaviness, a sense of hopelessness I couldn't describe. I knew in my heart drugs were involved, without it being said. My feelings of devastation were coupled with the reality that if I didn't stop, I would be joining Whitney in death.

I was done.

Unfortunately, in that moment, I had too much money and too many drugs in front of me to stop right then. That was more powerful than any desire to quit. Six days and $3000 later, with nothing of material value left in my house besides the furniture. No baths, no food, and a case of severe dehydration, I came to view the shell of a person in the mirror. What I saw looking back at me represented death. I had been here before, but it seemed never to this extreme. A part of me was ready to die, the other was ready to surrender.

I made the call to my brother and told him I was ready. I packed my bag. We took the ride to the hospital pretty much in silence. They took me to the back and ran test. A couple of hours and two sandwiches later, the nurse stated I was being sent home due to having no beds available at this time. She advised that I try again in a couple of days.

Desperation kicked in.

I told her that if I went home, I would surely die. I meant it. I couldn't go back there.

They placed someone at my door and two hours later, stated they could admit me to detox. I agreed. I was unsure of the outcome, but I was willing. I'd tried everything I knew to try to stop using. Nothing worked. My life was in shambles.

I remember sleeping a lot and barely participating in the classes. When I felt I was being talked down to, I showed out. I was summoned to the office of one of the head people after slamming a door. The woman shared her story of overcoming addiction. She encouraged me to believe in myself because she believed in me. This conversation changed my perspective and my life. We attended NA and AA meetings while I was there. I had been to NA before but would not allow myself to admit that I was an addict.

This time I listened.

This time I identified.

This time I surrendered.

It was a relief to discover what my affliction was. I do not suffer from a moral deficiency after all. I have a disease. Knowing that, opened the door to recovery. Admitting it, allowed me to begin the road to recovery.

————

SEVEN YEARS LATER, MY LIFE HAS CHANGED DRAMATICALLY. IT HAS not been easy, but I can easily say it has been the best seven years of my life. In the beginning of my recovery, I mourned the loss of my friends—alcohol and cocaine. I found I had no coping skills and my social skills were inept. A lot of my issues beyond using were exposed. At times, I thought about returning to active addiction. Primarily out of the fear of the unknown and stepping into unfamiliar territory. Thankfully, I quickly cast those thoughts down. I do not want to go back to the self-inflicted pain or the pain I caused others.

I can be there for my family and I have regained their trust. I no longer take flight when things are not going my way. I pray about it, I talk about it, and I get into the solution. I have learned to face everything head on and just take it one day at a time. Because I'm perfectly flawed, I still sometimes make unwise decisions and self-centeredness resurfaces. However, God in His grace and mercy has allowed me to realize that the world doesn't revolve around me. Some days are better than others. I have learned to embrace my assets and my liabilities.

I realize that the battlefield is in my mind. Self-evaluation is a daily ritual along with prayer and meditation. God continues to deal with me in my right now mess while He so lovingly helps me walk through my past mess. Not to relive, but to recover. To gain understanding so that I may be able to become better and better I have become. I am a good steward over the things God has allowed me to keep and the things He has added. I live now through my relationship with Christ Jesus. Some have entrusted me to help walk them through their struggles in life. I am both honored and humbled.

I still have a long way to go, but I am not where I used to be, nor am I defined by my past. I am excited about what life has to offer, good, bad, and indifferent; knowing and understanding that all things are working together for the betterment of me. I am not too much concerned about my final destination, I am enjoying the journey and it continues...

# AUTHOR BIO: CHARNIECE HARRIS

Charniece Harris was born in Kansas City, KS but relocated to relocated to Kinston, NC where she was raised by her maternal grandparents. She is the mother of Ra'Mel Harris (deceased) and is the oldest of five siblings.

Harris' life has been one of challenges. She struggled with the disease of addiction for over 30 years and battled depression. Seven years ago, she entered into a 12-Step program and began her Road to Recovery. In 2012, she graduated from Fayetteville State University with a BS in Criminal Justice.

Harris currently works in the finance industry and is a successful entrepreneur. The evidence and recipient of God's grace, she shares freely her experience, strength, and hope with others. Dedicated to helping those afflicted with addiction; Harris sponsors several individuals in the program that saved her life. She resides in Greenville, NC with her dog, Hugs.

# LET'S MAKE A DEAL: THE PRICE TO SHINE!

## Roz. A. Gee

# CHAPTER 1

IMAGINE BEING THE SUBJECT OF A PRIVATE CONVERSATION, WHERE LIFE-altering decisions were being discussed about you, your livelihood, and your destiny. However, you weren't invited to the conversation. Perhaps this wouldn't be a problem if the outcome of those decisions stacked in your favor and to your benefit, but what happens when they are to your detriment? How would you feel about not having any input in the negotiation process, or the details of this deal?

A conference meeting was held in Heaven's command center with God and a few executive staff. Uninvited, the adversary encroaches the room and interrupts the agenda. God asks, "Where have you come from?"

He responded, "From earth, where I've been watching everything that's going on and seeking whom I may devour."

Then God places a proposition on the table, an interrogative that would change the entire discourse of the meeting. "Have you considered my good friend Job?"

The adversary counters by saying, "But you have put a hedge of protection around him, his family and everything he owns. You've blessed him lavishly beyond his wildest dreams. Take away those things, and he will utterly denounce you."

God replied, "We'll see. Go ahead—do what you want with all that is his. Just don't touch him."

Suddenly, an avalanche of calamity fell upon Job's life. One devastating occurrence after the other was being reported to him. His amassed fortune and possessions were completely wiped out. His entire family was killed. On another day, a follow-up conference meeting was held back in the Command Center, and this time the negotiation was targeted towards Job's health.

The adversary's argument was, "Anyone would do anything to save his life. But what do you think would happen if his health was taken away? Surely, he will denounce you."

"Go ahead—you can do what you like with him. But don't kill him."

With God's permission, Job was mercilessly struck with extreme physical affliction. But throughout all of this, he never spoke a word against God, nor did he renounce Him.

Here we recount a portion of the biblical narrative in the life of Job. He was living a prosperous life when he was abruptly dealt a barrage of devastating blows that altered his life's trajectory. Now, can you imagine his dilemma of being attacked by terror, gripped with fear, blindsided by trauma, drowning in depression and the hopeless feeling of being rejected, forsaken and abandoned by God?

Not only can I imagine, but I experienced it.

And not only did I experience it, I survived to tell the story.

———

ON THOSE COOL, AUTUMN NIGHTS DRIVING DOWN OLD LINTON HALL Road in Gainesville, Virginia. I was super excited to pull up to my brand-new townhome in the Kingsbrooke community. The year was 1997 and I was only 27 years old working for a top tech company, America Online (AOL) as a software quality engineer. My new route from work now seemed like a long one, since the area was rural compared to the neighboring city I moved from. There were a few light poles scattered along the dark two-lane road. Coming home was bittersweet, I was ecstatic because of being a new homeowner, even though the commute was oftentimes daunting.

I purchased and settled in October and by December during my evening commutes home, I literally felt weighted or overcome with some emotion like grief. I remember many times leaning into the steering wheel of my 1996 Acura Integra because the weight was so heavy. Although I'm unable to articulate it fully, it seemed like a dark cloud was lowering around me.

About one week into the new year, while in a sound sleep suddenly I was jolted awake and struck with terror. Immediately, I fell to the floor from a high 4-poster bed gasping for every breath. I couldn't fully process what I was experiencing at that moment, but it seemed as if I ran smack into the wrath of God. Between lying with my face pressed into the carpet and rocking back and forth on my knees, I began to fervently pray and ask God to forgive *every* sin I ever committed thinking I was at the door of death. In agonizing negotiation for my soul, there were repeated pleadings for mercy and desperate cries for help as I sobbed uncontrollably.

With just a few hours before daybreak, it felt like an eternity. Too afraid to leave while it was still dark, I couldn't wait for the light to pierce the darkness so I could flee from my house. Without giving prior notice, I jumped in my car and sped to my friends, Mark and Marcie's home who lived about 20 minutes away. They were top leaders in the church I attended.

I rang the doorbell and there I stood with uncombed hair, wearing dark red sweatpants and a green and white striped hoodie. After being invited to sit at the kitchen table, they could sense that something was wrong. Mark placed his bible on the table, and proceeded to ask what was going on? My voice began to shake, and my speech became incoherent. I was searching for the words to describe the strike of terror that occurred during my sleep. As I did, I was gripped with overwhelming fear and I lost it—I lost control. On the kitchen floor with my back pressed against the dishwasher, my hands and legs were in motion involuntarily. And that's when I would later discover, that I was experiencing an anxiety and panic attack. Crying hysterically while Marcie was consoling me, praying for me, holding me. Many months later, she told me that the dishwasher wasn't working at the time, but I apparently shook it up a little—and caused it to work again!

The next thing I recall was my mother on the phone. When I heard Momma's voice, it was as if I was hearing it for the first time, and the last time. The sound of her voice brought instant relief, as I attempted to compose myself to carry on a conversation. "Rosalyn...Rosalyn?" She continued to call out to me until she got a response. She instructed me to call on the name of Jesus and to say it repeatedly. I did. My mother was coaching and praying on my behalf, and that critical moment reinforced our bond as mother-daughter. I didn't want to disconnect from the call, being certain that this would be our last conversation. So, I ended with, "I love you Momma."

Someone called 9-1-1, and that made me nervous and borderline angry. First, because it confirmed that something abnormal was really going on and secondly, it fed into a false fear that if I go to the hospital, I wasn't coming back—I would die. When the paramedics arrived, the team was courteous and professional, this was important since this was the first time being transported by ambulance.

Once onsite, they administered the normal routine, vitals checks, bloodwork, IV connection, etc. Shortly thereafter, a doctor came in and asked a series of questions that seemed like a cross-examination in the court of law. More time elapsed until I was transported to the Center for Psychiatric and Drug Treatment.

I was taken aback, and kept thinking, "Well, I'm not on drugs, neither do I have a history with drugs or psychiatric issues so why am I being taken here." Thankfully, the facility name has been completely changed to include Behavioral Health.

During the intake process, it seemed like the same battery of questions were being asked by different medical professionals all day. I was becoming more and more weary in answering the questions because of physical exhaustion and lack of sleep. My close circle of friends were right by my side. My body continued to do its own thing—sitting down, standing up, and clapping my hands in rapid succession. I tried to clutch them with all my might to stop but to no avail. The staff kept asking if I was in any physical pain, and my response was consistently no. But I was fighting, my spirit was fighting to stay alive. Battle weary and exhausted, I collapsed in a chair. Marcie had on a purple hat that she placed on my head, which immediately gave me a sense of dignity and permission to rest. It was a beautiful act of love.

Finally, after being assigned to a room and getting acclimated to the facility, I encountered a friendly lady (whose name I can't recall but I will call her Tina) in one of the common areas. Tina began to share a little about herself, and I honestly don't know if I was listening from sheer excitement that I found someone to connect with and didn't have to feel alone. She suggested that we meet later that evening for a bible study. I gleefully agreed. After settling into my room, I circled back to the common area and there she was. When I went to greet her, she looked at me strangely. So strangely until I went on to remind her that we met just a few hours earlier. With a puzzled look, she re-introduced herself with an entirely new name! Of course, I was waiting for a punch line of, "I'm just kidding." But when I realized her demeanor, voice and attitude had completely shifted; frozen right there on the spot, I broke down and cried because I thought a) that this was some malicious game or conspiracy, b) I was losing my mind and c) "she" was me and I just didn't know it! After having such a traumatic and stressful day, the evening ended leaving me more anxious and more fearful. Suddenly, I didn't feel safe and I kept questioning myself asking what was happening to me, and where was I.

The next day, Tina approached me and asked what happened to our meeting for bible study last evening. I was floored. When I explained that I did show up, but she was "someone else" that's when she began to disclose her condition. I would soon learn that she had multiple personalities. Today, it's called dissociative identity disorder. Formerly known as multiple personality disorder, this disorder is characterized by "switching" to alternate identities. Each identity may have a unique name, personal history and characteristics, including obvious differences in voice, gender, mannerisms and even such physical qualities such as wearing eyeglasses. Tina had 16 different personalities that formed after being sexually abused by her father for many years since her youth. The personalities were a coping mechanism to escape from the pain and reality of her abuse.

IN DISORDERS SUCH AS THESE, FEAR CAN SURFACE AND SHOW UP IN many different facets or faces and places. You may have heard that fear is an acrostic for "false evidence appearing real." It is true. Fear will attempt to "disorder" your identity suggesting that you believe a reality that is not true, falsified, or made up. It comes to cripple you from taking the next step, from moving forward—in your goals, purpose, dreams and destiny. Faith is the ultimate antidote to fear. Throughout this ordeal thus far, I feared the worse but none of those things came to fruition.

# CHAPTER 2

AFTER BEING HOSPITALIZED FOR ABOUT SEVEN DAYS, I WAS RELEASED to go home. During my time there, nothing substantial came out of the diagnosis, they couldn't find anything wrong except for a urine infection which I was prescribed an antibiotic but no other medication. Although I was pleased to be released, I was absolutely dreading going back to my new townhome. I was so convinced in my mind that it was the townhouse that had something to do with the night terror I experienced. Being a single woman, I certainly didn't want to stay there alone. My parents kept telling me to sell it especially if it was causing me this much grief. It was awful. At that time, I sorely regretted my decision to purchase the home. Since then I've learned that my home wasn't the problem but was only a trigger for the traumatic experience that occurred there. It wasn't the house; it was the pain associated with the house.

Going into the third week post-release, my wellbeing dwindled drastically. With a loss of appetite, I was not eating, resting or sleeping at all. Extreme sadness developed into full-blown depression. I returned to work, but totally unproductive, my boss was aware of my condition and allowed me to close my office door all day. Wondering how long could or would this go on, I witnessed one day rolling into the next. A big concern was how much could my physical body withstand before breaking down. Honestly, my condition was extremely taxing on my close circle of friends but in my state of desperation, I was always on a quest to find "who could I spend the night with next?"

Intense loneliness and isolation seemed to envelope me while it appeared as if everyone was turning away one-by-one. Perhaps my condition was becoming a weighted liability. No matter how much I tried to articulate, no one could understand or identify what I was going through. It was almost like I wanted them to experience what I was feeling on the inside. There wasn't a hug, smile, affection expression or prayer that made me feel any better. This was the first time in my life when I realized that you could hurt in another realm of your being, an unseen realm—your soul. A place where no doctor, no medical procedure, no physical test could detect that pain let alone provide a remedy. Suspended between time and eternity, no one was coming to my rescue. Where was God in all of this?

———

WEEKS PASSED BY AND STILL NO SLEEPING, RESTING OR EATING. I dropped a substantial amount of weight. Although there were people all around, I felt cut off from the rest of humanity, forsaken by God. I kept searching for answers, specifically what I did to deserve this. I lost my zeal for life, even though I was breathing but existing without purpose, value or significance. One Sunday while at church, I was hurting so bad on the inside, so I requested to see the pastor. Desperately wanting him to empathize with my inner anguish, I became overly emotional and signs of anxiety re-surfaced right there on the spot. My parents were called, despite my earnest pleas not to contact them because I knew what that meant, I was going back to the facility. And that's exactly what happened.

———

IT WAS NOW FEBRUARY, I REALLY RESENTED BEING READMITTED AND was still a little perturbed with my parents for sending me back. It was like I didn't belong there, like an illegal alien, a foreigner. When it came time to introduce myself during a group session, I remember how embarrassed I was to disclose that I was an engineer working for a high-profile IT company. I presumed that professionals weren't admitted to facilities like these especially after hearing some of the heart-wrenching stories from people who were addicted to heroin, alcohol and had ultra-traumatic childhoods or occurrences. Listening to their stories made me question if they were making this stuff up, it seemed surreal. In my naivety, I was just a country girl reared in rural North Carolina to a middle-class family, largely sheltered from societal ills.

During group sessions, I was tempted on a few occasions to alter my story to include hardships so that I would be accepted by the group. My "perfect" story of being a first-family college grad, working as an engineer in a coveted company, buying a new home and suddenly suffering from anxiety and depression just didn't seem to measure up. One man openly expressed his frustration towards me with screams of angry outbursts because he felt I was withholding the truth about why I was admitted to the facility. It was extremely challenging to process what happened to me, let alone articulate it in an open group setting. It seemed unfair to those who were sharing their life stories and this further caused me to shrink and feel unqualified to be there.

As a patient, I was assigned to a psychiatrist and prescribed medication called Paxil, used to treat clinical depression and anxiety disorders. While Paxil has proven effective in treating these disorders, side effects in some patients have caused medical professionals to stop using the drug. It was recalled. GlaxoSmithKline was reprimanded by the U.S. Food and Drug Administration (FDA) for marketing Paxil as a valid treatment for children under the age of 18. It is now known that this drug can increase suicidal thoughts and actions in this age group which is the basis for many lawsuits. After I was discharged, I was instructed to continue to see the psychiatrist to monitor my progress and medication effectiveness. Eventually, I stopped using the medication altogether due to the side effects I was experiencing.

I wrestled with showing up for follow-up appointments, not because I didn't want to get help but because of the stigma associated with going to see a "shrink." Secondly, I felt that it was a conflict of my faith (religious values)—holding to the belief that if you had to see a psychiatrist, psychologist, counselor or go to therapy, that you weren't operating in faith. This is still an ongoing dilemma in the faith-based community, which is why many don't get the help they need. The stigma that continues to plague the African American and faith-based communities is being addressed. I've since learned that regardless of your religious background, God still uses medical professionals and practices to provide effective solutions in mental health. Today, I appreciate all the advocacy and support efforts to de-stigmatize the issues around mental health and provide breakthroughs for those suffering in silence.

# CHAPTER 3

BACK AT HOME, THE ANXIETY ATTACKS SUBSIDED BUT I WAS LEFT IN deep depression and brokenness. Feeling powerless, I couldn't even pray or stay focused enough to read scripture. Instead of asking where was God, the real question was where was my faith? It was like I was spiritually shipwrecked. It was disappointing because I felt like I should have been stronger in my response during my trial. Insomnia, extreme fear, intense loneliness and isolation, worthlessness, and no desire to live were the dominant realities daily. Even the food I consumed had zero taste and provided no pleasure. I kept thinking is this what it's like without God? Life had no meaning. Life had no pleasure. Life had no significance. Life had no point! It was awful, just awful. At this point, I didn't care if I lived or died and often had visions of my funeral so vividly.

One day, my Daddy drove up from North Carolina to come get me. I will never forget how loving, supportive and encouraging he was. I told him that I didn't want to live any longer. He scolded me and told me to never say that again. After that, I stopped crying and cheered up some, and we had a good conversation heading back to Carolina. After spending a week with my parents and siblings, it was refreshing. There's no place like home. There is nothing like a parent's unconditional love. The time of retreat reminded me of the value and bond of family. How family stands for and supports you even in the darkest and lowest moments of your life. For that, I will always be grateful.

———

During this bazaar season of testing, I spent a considerable amount of time in deep reflection, and the biggest epiphany was discovering a deeper meaning of life. I saw things for what they truly were. What I placed value on: career, home, amenities, stock portfolio and the like paled in comparison to the priceless intangibles: inner peace, soundness of mind, contentment, rest/sleep, happiness, joy and the ability to enjoy the simple pleasures of life. Above all, having a right relationship with God which is all-encompassing and all-satisfying. It's the goodness of God that causes us to enjoy life!

I had been attending a small, start-up church that met in an industrial office park. After service, one of the ladies, Diana, was concerned that I didn't look my usual self but appeared spaced out and disoriented. It deeply disturbed her to the point where she was heartbroken and cried for hours that day. The following week on a bright, sunny afternoon, I was sad sitting on the kitchen floor. The hardwood was gleaming so beautifully as the sunlight beamed through the front windows. And for the first time, I entertained suicidal thoughts. To be clear, I wasn't plotting or planning to take my life, but wanted to be out of this world. This trial was too heavy to bear. I had no intention to harm myself but just wanted to stop hurting. While those negative thoughts were lingering, the doorbell rang. This was unsuspecting because I wasn't expecting any guests.

When I went to answer the door, there stood Diana from my church. I don't recall ever being so happy to see someone. It was like an angel showed up to my door. She went on to express that she was extremely concerned after seeing the state I was in. These were some of the side effects of taking Paxil. We talked for a while, and her genuine compassion was contagious. I felt safe. Then she abruptly said, "let's go, you are not staying here by yourself." She didn't have to tell me twice, I packed my bag and headed out the door. What a relief to leave and be with somebody—anybody. I just didn't want to be at home alone.

Originally, I thought I'd stay a few days, no more than a week to pull myself together and completely regroup. Well, a week quickly turned into 3 months! Living with Diana and her three daughters was the beginning to a long road of recovery. We lived in tight living quarters, three small bedrooms and one shared bath. I didn't complain whatsoever but was grateful to be a part of a safe community with my new family.

Diana encouraged me to stay for as long as I needed to. Her graciousness, hospitality and selflessness left an indelible mark on my life. Although, she never disclosed this, extending my stay was a huge risk because she was a part of a subsidized housing program. She cared for me day and night. I stopped taking the medication and showing up for weekly therapy appointments because I felt my progress wasn't improving. So, I was still clinically depressed and lethargic.

Some major breakthroughs occurred; the return of my appetite, the ability to eat and the ability to sleep and get a good night's rest!

Finally, I was beginning to see rays of light peeking through this dark abyss. It was an uphill battle from here. Many days I struggled to get out of bed, my good night's rest turned into wanting to sleep all the time. This is where my relationship with Diana would be tested. To ensure that I didn't miss going to work. She would force me to take a shower, get dressed, brush my teeth, and comb my hair. It was the same routine that she did with her youngest daughter.

This annoyed me to no end! She did whatever was necessary to keep me moving forward in the mornings—even if it meant spraying my linen and pillowcases with shave cream so that I wouldn't return to bed. Then she would literally push me out the door and lock it, leaving no choice for me but to go to work. These shenanigans occurred day after day, and there were occasions where we would borderline fight because I refused to cooperate with getting my day started.

These were some of the behaviors that accompanied clinical depression. There are several symptoms, but one is a lack of motivation to do basic activities. Some people stay in their homes or a specific room in their home and refuse to come out. Some keep the blinds closed and curtains drawn for weeks and months. Some withdraw from other people altogether. Some have overwhelming sadness or despair. Millions of people in America and around the globe suffer with some form of depression. Its purpose is to keep you "pressed" down and debilitated. The good news is that you don't have to stay gripped in its' clutches.

There is a plethora of resources available such as contacting the National Alliance on Mental Illness at 800-950-NAMI or visiting www.NAMI.org. It's also critical to develop a support system that may include a family member or friend that you can trust. You do not have to walk out this process alone.

As each month went by living with my new family, more healing began to take place. Finally, I regained my strength, confidence and desire to move forward. Getting back into the flow of a daily regimen and performing normal activities independently were positive indicators that the nightmare I'd been living was coming to an end. There were no signs of anxiety, fear or symptoms of depression. It was a beautiful thing to see my life coming into full view. The sun shone a little brighter. My smile stretched a little wider. There was a little more pep with every step. In the spring of June 1998, I decided to face my giant and muster the courage to return home. I decided to move my life forward. So, I gathered all my belongings, and moved back to my new abode. I was looking forward to settling into a new life, a life free from oppression and bondage.

In hindsight, throughout this whole ordeal God was carrying me the entire time. One thing I knew for sure, if God didn't deliver me, I wouldn't be delivered. There was no single thing that I did to cure what was ailing me. All the credit belongs to God. It never ceases to amaze me of His steadfast love and faithfulness. The way He brought me through was so skillful, strategic and seamless until it was almost undetectable.

In life, we may have traumatic events happen without knowing why, but there are lessons to be learned if we're open to be taught. We must search for the good amid the bad. Some of my lessons include how powerless we are without the intervention of God. How priceless it is to live in a state of perpetual peace. How precious relationships are

—when people go above and beyond to love you in low places. How we are much stronger than we think we are, it's the testament of the power of the human spirit.

My aunt, whom I refer to as my bonus mom, prayed earnestly for me, and shared that God didn't reveal to her why I was going through this trial, only that it would be glorious. This really encouraged my heart and gave me hope even after 21 years. To know what I suffered wasn't in vain but God would somehow use it for His glory was like a balm to my soul. In other words, what was intended for evil, He would bring good out of it. We are resilient and no matter how much darkness we may be encapsulated in, the light of our spirit will always emerge. There is an illuminating essence within to shine!

Although I never really understood *why* the series of events occurred, I only know that they did occur. In retrospect, it has made me a better person, a stronger person, one that's more aware of what really matters in life. So, the question becomes, what was I supposed to learn and gain from these experiences? This experience has revealed that the most valuable and prized possession is your soul. Your soul makes up your mind, will and emotions. Having all the accoutrements of life and success certainly has its place but there is nothing more priceless than an undisturbed soul—that includes the gift of peace, a sound mind, and balanced emotional health. It causes you to re-evaluate the things we take for granted everyday—such as our ability to get a good night's sleep, to think rationally and make sound decisions, and to live in freedom from fear. The simplest of things such as enjoying a meal or thinking happy thoughts or breathing in fresh air. The fondest of things such as a friend showing up to support you during your darkest hour, going the extra mile to make sure that you are okay, or simply praying on your behalf. These are the underlying sparks that cause a life to illuminate and radiate perpetually.

My story is a testament of how a disruptive trial can be used to transcend darkness into light. I pray I'll be able to help others who have experienced similar traumatic events so that they, too, won't have to suffer in silence. When anyone goes through something of similar magnitude, it doesn't seem as if there is an exit or way of escape. There is a scripture that reminds us, *no temptation has overtaken you* *except what is common to mankind. And God is faithful; he will not let you be tempted beyond what you can bear. But when you are tempted, he will also provide a way out so that you can endure it (*I Corinthians 10:13).

For those who are deeply discouraged or rapidly losing hope, who feel trapped in the abyss of uncertainty. Know that what you're experiencing or have experienced is not the end of your story, it's a chapter or two in your full book of life. Just like in the ending story of Job, he was restored double of everything that he lost! It's evidenced that the brightest lights can emerge from the deepest darkness. Plus, I believe that there will be recompense and restoration of what we have suffered. We may not know in what form it will come back, or how it will be measured or quantified. What was intended for our destruction, will work purposely for our transformation, elevation and illumination.

*Shine* on.

# AUTHOR BIO: ROZ A. GEE

After navigating and surviving more than a decade of a downward spiral, Roz A. Gee discovered that she is the irrefutable proof of her own story. She's on a mission to help others embrace the reality that they too, are the *Evidence*.

A native of coastal, southeastern North Carolina, alumni of Fayetteville State University, and member of Alpha Kappa Alpha Sorority, Roz and James currently resides in the Washington, DC metropolitan area.

As the owner of a media and branding firm, The Rated Gee Agency, LLC (www.RatedGee.com), Roz is a published author, speaker, media consultant and contributor working with high-achieving business leaders, influencers and celebrities. Her work has been featured in *Gospel Today*, B*lack Enterprise*, *ESSENCE, Ebony, American Express, INC. Magazine, The Huffington Post, FOX and ABC.*

Follow on Facebook: RozAGee
Follow on Instagram: IAmRozGee
Follow on Twitter: IAmRozGee

# AGAINST ALL ODDS

## Lisa Thomas-Lewis

# CHAPTER 1

"YOU ARE NEVER GOING TO GET YOUR TOE SHOES IF YOU KEEP eating... keep being mouthy and see what's going to happen to you... you can do anything Lisa, just keep making honor roll and the sky is the limit for you... self-preservation... self, self, self, and self again— then your friend..."

These were affirmations my mother spoke over my life. Good or bad—it all came to pass one way or another. Little did I know then that you can literally speak life and death over someone because it's all in the power of the tongue.

I was taught self-preservation by an incredibly strong black woman. It wasn't that I was taught to be selfish, but I was taught the importance of taking care of yourself and home first. I didn't always follow mom's rules of thumb and when I didn't, it cost me some unwanted trouble. The saying: "A hard head makes a soft behind" was very true. Mom was always right 99% of the time, although I hated to admit it.

*Married but Single* was not only a famous stage play—it was the scenario that played throughout my life as I witnessed the unconventional and toxic union between my parents which lasted for close to 20 years. Because I was raised in a two-parent home, I thought that I was living my best life back in the 70's. I had a mixture of friends who were raised in two-parent households like myself; however there were some raised by single parents. There were times when I believed that the households with single moms were better off than those of us who lived with both parents.

I can say this with conviction because my mother was truly the epitome of a strong black woman. She made sure all four of her children had everything we needed. However, my father was the stepfather to my three siblings and even though I came from a household that appeared to be well put together: both my parents had college degrees and great jobs; however, we were still living in a toxic and unfulfilled environment. On the outside it looked as if everything was fine; truly an example of public success but within the home, our lives were a private failure.

My father was never home. He was constantly working or running the streets. He had a habit of disappearing for weeks at a time, and when he eventually came home, his presence would ignite a constant flow of arguments.

My mother sacrificed and would do anything for her children. Additionally, she was a community leader, a career professional and a community activist. I watched my mother very closely while I was growing up. All she really wanted was to have a happy home without drama—something that didn't appear to be possible in my household. However, she never gave up. She was the epitome of Wonder Woman.

She always taught me to be a person of integrity. I was the only girl amongst my brothers and the youngest, so she also instilled in me the importance of being self-sufficient. Mom was the baby on both sides of her family because both of her parents had been previously married with children prior to their union. I always felt such a spiritual connection with my mother because we had so many things in common; like being the youngest amongst our siblings and being the leaders amongst our friends and family with an amazing ability to be strong.

My mother used to always tell me that I was always trying to save people and I needed to learn to take care of myself first. I had always watched her put others first so I did the same. Throughout my life I saw my mom be the perfect soccer mom although my brothers played a variety of sports such as football, baseball and wrestling. She was the ultimate team mom; feeding them and doing fundraisers. I found myself following in her footsteps with my own children. She was my role model. Unfortunately, I also found myself reliving some portions of her life that may or may not have been conducive for her health or mine.

Because of her training and words of wisdom, I refused to settle for certain attributes in a man such as being lazy, having no vision about the future and flat out not being compassionate or considerate of other people feelings. I knew I wanted a husband who would be a hard worker and provide for our family. However, there were certain attributes that I didn't know to pray for in a husband.

My mother had been a mom since she was 15. She was book smart but not street smart. She built and bought her first home at the age of 19 during a time when African Americans were severely struggling. Back then, due to women inequalities and the fact that she hadn't turned 21 yet when she purchased our home, my mom faced many discriminatory issues.

On the day of her closing, she had to have her attorney put the house in his name until she became of age because they were leery of the fact that she was a young unmarried woman with children.

Nevertheless, she persevered and when she turned 21, the house was placed solely in her name. It has been this type of tenaciousness that my mother demonstrated throughout my life which kept me going whenever I was confronted with different tragedies.

My mother was a natural leader and a pillar in our local community. It was through her I learned about politics. I remember when Jesse Jackson ran for President of the United States—my mother was part of his local campaign team in Michigan. I remember being at the campaign headquarters working, folding letters and sealing envelopes.

I soon realized that Mom stayed busy to mask the emotional pain that she often felt due to her toxic relationship with my dad. I can imagine that her turbulent marriage, raising children at such a young age was very challenging and overwhelming. My oldest brother lived with my grandmother. We considered him the lucky one because he didn't have to experience the constant fighting which took place in our *perfect* home.

Going to my grandmother's home, which was technically around the corner from our house was like going to a resort on a daily basis because there we could have peace of mind.

My grandmother also taught us many life skills growing up. We learned how to cook, clean, work in the hot sun in the garden pulling tomatoes and vegetables and tilling the soil.

My mother was not much of an outdoors person. She was a diva back in the day, so getting her hands dirty was out of the question. Thank God for my grandmother because of her—I know how to be a lady, not be afraid to get my hands dirty, clean up and keep it moving. The irony is that my mom knew how to work on cars, build a house and put up drywall, yet when it came to gardening—it was not her cup of tea.

My mother had a mind for business. She was an entrepreneur and a true visionary. She not only worked in corporate America, she was also a licensed cosmetologist who ran a hair salon from our home. She also owned an event planning and catering company where she catered large weddings and various company events within the automotive industry and other professional clientele.

She always worked hard but she literally enjoyed making other people happy. She was also the life of the party whenever she would "let her hair down." This didn't happen too often for her because she was constantly working and trying to make sure that her family was taken care of. She always seemed to be in survival mode because she loved having the finer things in life, but she always had to work hard to attain them and working hard was a characteristic that she demonstrated to her children.

Throughout my mother's life journey, she always made it a priority to keep not only her immediate family unit together but also our extended family. Mom was the coordinator of our family reunions for over 25 years. She made sure that we had beautiful reunions in different states and venues every year. Because my grandmother was married three different times, our family was huge, and my mother spent a great portion of her life trying to find relatives from the South who had not matriculated to the North. Due to my mother's research, she was able to locate hundreds of family members we never knew about and in 2008, we made a memorable trip to Alabama to bring the families together.

However, due to cancer my mother passed before getting to see the full fruit of what that foundational trip to Alabama created for future family reunions and connections.

One thing I admired most about my mom is the way she carried herself through the bad times as well. Her marriage was a turbulent one, but she refused to drown herself in misery. She held her head up high and focused on her children.

I fashioned my life after her, even in my marriage. Living with a man battling alcohol abuse has not been an easy road to travel. There have been many times when I've wanted to give up the fight and just move on with my life—just focus on my children. During those times, I would reflect on my mother and the way she persevered. Talking to her and soaking up her wisdom renewed my strength. Her advice kept me on the right path. She was there for me in so many ways—she would sit for hours listening to me vent, scream, cry, whatever… She was mom.

# CHAPTER 2

DEATH COMES TO EACH OF US INEVITABLY, BUT I WAS NOT READY TO say goodbye to my mother. I needed her calming words of wisdom, her wonderful hugs and her delightful smile. Just seeing her would make my world a better place in that special moment. Her passing left me feeling abandoned and angry. I had no support and I felt as if everyone expected me to just get on with life—I grieved deeply. I was alone and dying inside; nobody seemed to notice or care, planting seeds of bitterness within.

During her lifetime, Mom taught me so much. How to ride the storms of life; how to be a good mother; how to stand up after being knocked down... but there was one crucial thing she didn't teach me—how to live without her. She was my voice of reason; the moral compass whenever I wanted to skid off the rails. How was I supposed to survive losing her?

Her death taught me some important things. Though my life has been oftentimes like the three Hebrew boys in the fiery furnace, God has allowed me to come out of the fire without any spot or wrinkle. I've learned that we are all perfectly flawed—perhaps some more than others, but flawed, nonetheless. Marriage is hard work, but I had to remember that it should be a three-strand cord (me, my husband and

God). Mom taught me to never underestimate the power of a praying wife. There are times I went into battle within my marriage—times when I should have been going to war for my marriage. Then there are the instances when I have to step aside, and watch God work. I've learned that every broken heart has a healing process. My heart included.

All the blessings from God have come about in my life because Mom taught me to turn it all over to the Lord and release the hurt and pain of wanting to be angry at everybody.

———

HAVING A BIG HEART TOWARDS OTHERS, WHETHER THEY ACKNOWLEDGE it or not makes you an ambassador for Christ. I realize now how much mercy God granted my mother and how He covered her life with all types of favor because she served and worshipped Him. I thank God Mom taught me to do the same and I'm now teaching my children to love and worship the Lord. It has been this same amazing love and God's Grace that allows me to forgive so that my blessings can continue to overflow in my life.

Finally, my mother and father both taught me endurance and the true forgiveness that was experienced on the cross by Jesus. Just like in his last moments and how he cried out in Luke 23:34, *"forgive them father for they know not what they do."*

I learned to grow in this same sacrificial love and live the prophetic last words of my mother "All is well."

# AUTHOR BIO: LISA THOMAS-LEWIS

Lisa Thomas-Lewis is an author, speaker and financial consultant who lives her life as a purpose-driven woman of God passionate about helping others to evolve and live a life of abundance. A native of the Metro Detroit area in Michigan, Lisa graduated from Hampton University in Virginia where she earned a BS in Accounting and an MBA in Strategic Management from Davenport University. She is a taskmaster and professional motivator at helping people to maximize their life experiences. She is the CEO of LRT and Associates, LLC and Legacy Lessons with Lisa, LLC. When she finds time to relax, Lisa enjoys spending time with her family, attending sporting and music events and traveling abroad.

Email: shinewithlisat@gmail.com
Instagram: Lisa Thomas-Lewis
Twitter: @MzProf_Consult
Facebook: Lisa Thomas-Lewis

# FREEDOM THROUGH FORGIVENESS

## Katonya Freeman

# CHAPTER 1

## Born by Choice & Raised with Love

KaTonya is my name but he called me Tonya D and dear heart. My mom became pregnant with me while in school. My dad would leave love notes and her favorite candy in her locker. He would do sweet little things like this for her. She always talked about how athletic he was—it was obvious how much she loved him. I loved listening to the stories about their relationship.

When she discovered she was pregnant—she had a decision to make because back then, the school system didn't allow expectant students to attend class. My mom had to decide whether to terminate her pregnancy or keep me.

She chose me.

My dad was able to continue his education and graduate because my mom told them that he was not the father of her child. He wouldn't have been able to stay in school either had they known the truth.

After my birth, I was surrounded by love, and was a spoiled by my grandmother and aunt. When I was in Headstart, I used to love it when my aunt took me to school in her green Pontiac with the black stripes on the hood. That was one cool car to me. She would even pick up my friend.

I also used to love to watch my mother dance. She was a fantastic dancer and I often tried to mimic her moves. I loved life and I loved my family.

Most importantly, I knew I was loved.

# CHAPTER 2

## Good Times but Something Just isn't Right

MY ELEMENTARY AND MIDDLE SCHOOL AGE DAYS WERE GOOD TOO. WE were living in an apartment and I was loving life. My grandmother would get up every Sunday morning and listen to the Andy Herring radio show. She cooked with gospel music playing in the background.

I often woke up to the mouthwatering smell of collard greens, ham, fried chicken, corn bread and homemade cakes. My grandmother had Sunday dinner prepared by the time her ride picked us up for church.

I spent my summer and winter breaks with my father and his family. They often spoiled me as well. As a child, I felt life was great. I only saw the good in people—I viewed life through the perspective of a child who was loved and nurtured by the adults in his or her environment. I felt safe and secure.

My paternal grandmother taught me how to shell peas and shuck corn during my visits with my father. I enjoyed shucking corn under the big tree near her garden but I must confess that I never liked shelling beans because they hurt my fingers.

My father loved music and could play different instruments. I love singing and music also. He showed me where different parts of the car was and what it was for. I learned how to check the oil and water. I remember feeling proud that he was teaching me things about a car at such a young age.

Christmas was always a special time for my father's family. We would go shopping for a tree to decorate. My dad's sister would take me to purchase gifts for everyone. As I mentioned earlier—life was great.

I never imagined that I would ever feel differently.

# CHAPTER 3

## Red Flags

THERE WAS A POINT IN MY LIFE WHEN I BEGAN TO FEEL UNEASY around a certain family member. Initially, I didn't understand why, but he made me uncomfortable whenever he came around. He would want hugs I never wanted to give. I often found myself trying to avoid him if at all possible.

I can't say whether it was a vibe he was giving off or just the instincts of a child, but I didn't care to be in the same room with this person, despite him being a member of my family. Any touch on my shoulder or arms irritated me—I felt as if he'd invaded my personal space.

There was one incident when I had to sit close to him. He pulled me back against him so that I was positioned between his legs. He held me in a tight grip so I couldn't move away. It just didn't feel right to me. However, I never mentioned how this person made me feel to my mother. I didn't understand it myself, so how could I explain it to her?

---

MY MOM KEPT US IN CHURCH. WE USE TO GO SO MUCH THAT KIDS called me *Church Lady*. I hated being called that name and having to wear dresses all the time until Jr High School. We would go in my mom room at six in the evening to pray.

As I became older, I understood and really appreciated everything my mom taught me about faith. The prayers she taught me helped me in my silent angst.

# CHAPTER 4

## Betrayed

My world changed New Year's Eve.

I was in the living room watching television when this person came in and sat down beside me. At the time, I didn't think much of it—I didn't exactly want any company while I watched Dick Clark's show, but I wasn't bothered by his presence until he wanted to sidled close to me.

He suddenly leaned over me and kissed my neck really hard. I was shocked and terrified. I'm sure he saw the fear in my eyes, but I could tell he didn't care. He was intent on getting what he wanted. I lay there paralyzed with terror as he molested me.

When it was over, I retreated as fast as I could to the bathroom. I looked in the mirror and saw red marks on my neck. My heart racing, I tried to think of how I could escape. I was afraid he'd come back and hurt me again. I couldn't go to a neighbor's house because everyone was either related or friends of the family. I didn't want to risk everyone finding out what happened—I hadn't fully processed it myself.

The one thing I knew for sure is that I no longer felt safe. A part of my soul had been tarnished and I'd been betrayed by a member of my family. In my naïveté, I 'd believed that family was supposed to protect —not violate.

# CHAPTER 5

I TOLD MY MOM WHAT HAPPENED.

She called him and told him what I had said, but he didn't want to talk. My mom was going to call the police on him, but I pleaded with her to keep them out of it. I didn't want to be a topic in the newspaper or on the TV news. I didn't want anyone to know what had happened to me.

Other family members began calling—apparently, he'd made some calls instead of talking to my mom. There was drama. I developed a headache and didn't want to talk to anyone. I was still trying to process the fact that I'd been victimized.

Because it had happened at the hands of a close member of my family—a line was drawn in the sand when it came to family loyalties. There were those who chose to believe his lies and ignore my truth. I was cut off from those members for years.

I was old enough to know that what he did was wrong. There was a moment when I wished I'd just let my mom call the police on him. Once again, he'd betrayed me by trying to paint me as a liar to other family members instead of discussing the truth with my mom. Perhaps it could've just stayed between the three of us.

He deserved to be punished, but instead he tried to punish me for speaking up. Despite everything, I'm glad I was brave enough to tell someone—tell my mother that someone I trusted had sexually abused me.

There is victory in not keeping his secret, albeit a small one.

———

A FEW YEARS AFTER MY HIGH SCHOOL GRADUATION. I HEARD FROM someone on that side of the family. We had a great conversation. The person who molested me came up in name only and I asked for his number. I was ready to have a conversation with him.

I called him. He was probably shocked to hear from me, but there was something I needed to say to him in order to fully heal. I told him that I forgave him from my heart and meant it.

On this particular day, after my conversation with him—I felt a total release and freedom. Without forgiveness, I wouldn't have been able to see him or discover he was a changed man. I wouldn't have been able to take him to get hot dogs. I wouldn't have been able to see him humble and caring. We stopped to the gas station after getting hot dogs and he helped a homeless couple. I found my peace in forgiving him. I had to take back what belonged to me. I was no longer a victim —I was victorious; an overcomer.

———

IF CHILDHOOD HURTS HAVE STOLEN YOUR JOY, PEACE, HAPPINESS AND freedom to live with a sound mind; remember that God has not given us the spirit of fear, but He has given us power. We have the power over the enemy. We have the keys called forgiveness. Everything that has ever happened in your life, now is the time to evict it out of your space. It wasn't meant to hurt you it was meant to destroy you. The hurt that they caused was just a stepping stone to cause you to become bitter, become like them and carry on the generational curses. The generational curse stops with you.

Get off that stone called hurt. It is time to step down and get in your rightful place. Show the weapon used to destroy your own life that it did not prosper. Renew your mind and read God's Word. The Word is God, so speak God into the atmosphere.

*I pray that my story helps you to overcome your past and use the key of forgiveness to regain your power. May God heal all of you wounds. I speak that the generational curses end now. I speak that your hurt will not control you anymore. I speak against all bitterness rooted in your heart. I pray for for supernatural healing in the hearts of your children and future generations. I speak that no weapon formed against you shall prosper. I pray that God will do a total detox in your body by taking away the taste for drugs, the thirst for alcohol. I pray against emotional eating and speak good health for your life. I pray against anxiety, depression, sexual perversion, mental illness and all things not of God. I speak total healing.*

*In Jesus' name*
*Amen*

- National Sexual Assault Hotline 800-656-4673
- National Suicide Prevention Hotline 1-800-273-8255
- National Human Trafficking Hotline 1-888-373-7888 sms: 233733 (text: HELP or INFO)
- Substance Abuse Helpline number 1-800-487-4889
- Mental Health Helpline 1-844-549-4266

# AUTHOR BIO: KATONYA FREEMAN

KaTonya Freeman is a native of Kinston NC Academy. She now resides in Raleigh, NC. KaTonya is the wife of Van Freeman and together, they are the proud parents of 7 children and 2 grandchildren. She is a servant, encourager, songwriter and author.

Evangelist KaTonya is a member of City of the Great King, where Dr. Marvin Smith is the pastor. She has served over the years as a youth leader, board of directors, planning committee and evangelistic team. She has been ordained in ministry and serves as Associate Pastor and Youth Pastor.

KaTonya's mantra is "KINGDOM MINDSET 100" Keep it going! With a Kingdom Mindset we have a mindset to please God and do His will 100%. Yet if we fall, we are to get back on course and keep it going. One of her favorite scriptures is Philippians 4:13 "I can do all things through Christ which strengthens me."

# BECOMING MOORE

## Rashonda Moore

# CHAPTER 1

I WAS THE OLDEST LIVING CHILD OF FIVE CHILDREN BECAUSE MY OLDER brother passed away at a very early age in a car driven by his father who survived the accident. I had memories of molestation as an adolescent. I always felt that somehow it was my fault.

My parents were married for close to 20 years. After they separated, my mother drove off into the sunset with four children to drive across country, relocating to another state. Upon arriving, she met an escort that would lead us the rest of the way to a shelter for battered women and children. It was tucked away and secluded within a very prestigious neighborhood.

Memories of early morning calls on an intercom alarming everyone in the shelter to get up. The children would get ready for the school bus to come and pick them up. Not much longer after being at the battered women's shelter, we moved to another before getting our own place within the Housing Authority.

This wasn't an easy transition for me. My mother often appeared sad and angry. I was too young to understand at the time, but my mother was depressed. She'd lost her firstborn son in an accident; the physical and verbal abuse she'd suffered throughout her marriage, infidelity, neglect, etc. As a matter of fact, neither of the parents went through any type of counseling after my brother's death and it had a huge impact and effect on all of us.

I recall the very early and inappropriate introduction to sex, an absent father along with my mother who was partially absent in the sense that she wasn't there to provide guidance to her children—she didn't teach us how to cook, clean, self-care, etc. There was so much I had to figure out on my own and I did.

I always questioned whether my mother loved me. I was often compared to my father whom was spoken of negatively. There were times I wondered if perhaps I'd been adopted because I couldn't understand how a mom could treat her daughter the way she treated me. Because of this—I felt the burden to prove my worth. I wanted to earn her love. I helped out as much as I could and even sold candy at school to make some extra cash. I worked my first job at the age of 14 and was able to buy my own school clothes, supplies and anything else I needed. I also contributed to the bills in the household as well, lessening the financial burden on my mother. I was even able to pay to have a personal phone line installed in my room.

I was raised as a Jehovah's Witness. I wasn't able to listen to certain types of music or watch certain television shows. My siblings and I played amongst ourselves—we didn't have any outside influences other than occasional visits to our cousin's house. Because we moved often—it was difficult to make friends at school. I grew up feeling lonely with no sense of belonging anywhere. I had nothing to which to compare my life situations, so it was my normal. However, as I think back, I realize my life at that time was not easy.

We moved again when I started high school. My siblings and I were able to make a few friends. We were allowed outside, but we had strict rules. Even with being told not to interact with others, eventually I piqued the interest of a certain young man at the apartment complex. He was persistent and soon we became involved. He was my first high school sweetheart.

I quit school after 10th grade. My mother was so invested in her new boyfriend that she didn't notice whether I went to school or not. I started out just skipping school a few times and eventually stopped going altogether.

Then my mother suddenly decided to move again—this time we were heading to Michigan. I was heartbroken at the thought of leaving my boyfriend behind. I didn't want to leave Georgia, but I had no choice in the matter.

Once we arrived—we were back in a shelter until my mother could find a place for us to live. I was intent on moving back to Georgia to be with the love of my life. My environment in Michigan could be described as turbulent at best. By the time I turned 16—I couldn't take any more. I bought a Greyhound Bus ticket and headed to Georgia. Leaving was bittersweet because I was leaving my siblings behind, who didn't want her to go.

I really wanted my mother to see me off, but she declined. Filled with hurt and disappointment, I called a cab, and headed to the bus station. When I arrived in Georgia, I stayed at a friend's house. This was short lived because within a few days of being there, the woman's older son, felt like he had a welcomed invitation to join her one night as she was sleeping.

I left there and went to stay with a family member. Living with them was for a FEE and not FREE. I was no stranger to work and began working that year for the AJC during the 1996 Olympic games in Atlanta with a friend from high school. 1996 was an eventful year. I experienced Freak Night for the first time, the 1996 Olympic Games, A Big Mike Tyson Fight, and Tupac's death all in the same year.

The night of the Mike Tyson Fight, another family member and I spent the night out. The next day I found all my belongings packed by the front door. In that moment, I had no other option but to leave, so I ended up at the Intown Suites, a weekly hotel.

This was wasn't the route I wanted to take for my life. I was constantly propositioned for sexual favors. After being taken advantage of by a Caucasian man staying there—I was ready to move on.

I called my boyfriend at the time and told him what happened. He asked his mother if I could stay there with them for a while. His mother allowed me to do so. I slept downstairs on a pullout bed. In the middle of the night, my boyfriend's brother made a pass at me. I told my boyfriend what happened which lead to a brawl between the brothers. I decided it was best to remove myself from this environment. I worked at Marshall's department store long enough to purchase a ticket to go to California where my mother and siblings lived.

Once there, I enrolled in a program to get my G.E.D. I took all the tests up front and passed above average in the same month and year I was supposed to graduate had I been in school. My intent was to return to Georgia after passing my test.

# CHAPTER 2

BACK IN GEORGIA, I FOUND A JOB WHERE I WAS SEXUALLY HARASSED by one of the managers. I found another job as a sales rep for a men's clothing store. During this time, me and a close friend decided to find a place together. By this time, I was 17 years old. A few months later, I bought my first car.

The roommate situation didn't last long, which left me needing to seek other alternatives. Simultaneously while this was going on, my mother and brother had moved back to Atlanta while my sister chose to remain on the West Coast. I moved in with my mom, but it was only going to be short-term. I planned to save enough money to secure my own place. I had to find another job, however. I had to find another job because of where we lived—it was too far to travel. I soon found another place of employment.

I enrolled in school to study Computer Science during the week and worked in the evenings and on weekends. I spent my free time with my boyfriend. When I was 21, he became the father of my first child. Although we were young, we were determined to be a family and raise our baby together.

He and I eventually moved into our own place. I had a very healthy pregnancy and worked all the way up until it was time for me to give birth. However, there were times when I was too tired to walk to the bus stop and my boyfriend wouldn't take her to work or to the train station. There were also times when I had doctor appointments and he didn't feel like taking me. I saw a change in him, and I didn't like it—he was not acting like a responsible expectant father should. I also discovered that he'd started selling drugs and often got frustrated when it time to pay the bills.

I ended up having to have labor induced because I was approaching 10 months and the baby was almost 10 pounds. The procedure began in the evening. Fourteen hours and 3 pushes later, my son was born 23.5 inches and 9.7 pounds. We went home two days later. I was happy with my little family.

It didn't last long.

Not too long after arriving to our place, the father of my newborn son announced that he was moving back home, and I should do the same. My emotions were all over the place—I'd just had a baby; the father wanted to run away, forsaking his child and the responsibilities that would come with raising a child. I'd worked hard to have my own home only to have to move back in with my mom.

A few months later, one of my sisters left California and moved in with us. I continued to work and take care of my son the best I knew how. Five months later, I was informed by my mother that she was moving again alone. My sister and I were left to find a place to stay.

My son's father caught the *let's make this work* bug, but I wasn't hearing it. My response was, "Help take care of your son; spend time with him but leave me out of it."

Over the years, I've reflected back on my life and wondered why members of my family weren't there to help guide me—a little guidance would have gone a long way. There was so much that I didn't know, and it took a few bumps, scrapes, scratches, and even some bruises before I was able to connect the necessary dots to make sense of my life. I learned that people can't give you something they weren't ever taught. It definitely took some time, but I was able to forgive everyone that had ever hurt me. Hurt people hurt people is not just a cliché–it is a fact. If you don't love yourself, you can never love anyone else. When you lack compassion, grace, love and mercy—you won't have any to give.

When you have been sexually abused even if it really didn't seem like abuse because of the familiar saying: "How can something that feels good be wrong?"

*It is wrong.*

Over a period of time, I've received apologies from most of the people who abused, neglected and misused her. I choose to embrace the positives in my life versus focusing on all the bad things that happened. I learned from my errors in judgement and mistakes. I learned how to make better choices and staying focused my goals. I learned not to give up; to smile in the face of bad times, but most of all —I realized that I could design my destiny one decision at a time and that I was created to *Shine*.

# AUTHOR BIO: RASHONDA MOORE

Rashonda Moore was born in Michigan, raised in California and is the oldest of four children with the same parents.

Initially skeptical about embracing and sharing a piece of the puzzle that is my life, Rashonda decided to write my truth with the intention and expectation of helping others. She found her healing in revealing personal vulnerabilities, hurts, and mistakes, but most importantly her triumphs.

Rashonda has been blessed with three beautiful children, a sound mind, an open heart to give & receive love, and a full understanding that she is perfectly imperfect; bruised but not broken and placed under pressure so that she can continue to shine.

# REDEEMED

## Detra Tyler

# CHAPTER 1

As a child growing up, I never felt like I fit in not even with my own family. I was the lighter child of all my cousins, aunts, uncles and my mom. I felt awkward in elementary school and I was picked on. At the time I didn't understand why but what I know now is as a child you want to fit in, you want friends and you want to be liked. I don't remember making a fuss about it I guess I just lived through it because I didn't really know that it should be different. I read a lot and often got lost in books by envisioning myself in the places I read about.

I remember planning to become a nurse and help people. I remember reading biographies about African American men and women that overcame great tragedies in life to gain a better life. I never knew as a child that I would face many disappointments and overcome obstacles myself as I got older. Most of the experiences I have had prior to writing my story, were preparing me for the moments ahead, I just didn't know it.

In middle school I got good grades and tried to stay out of trouble, but my town didn't have many activities outside of school that could keep me occupied. I did participate in basketball, cheerleading and softball. There was still opportunity for trouble, and it met me in varying ways. I got into fights often in middle school, I hated being the underdog having to always feel the need to prove myself through a fight, but that's how it was done in my neighborhood.

Girls don't like you; you fight! She thinks you like the same boy she likes; you fight! I grew up feeling that my presence made some of the girls in my neighborhood uncomfortable in some kind of way that was always translated by them just plain not liking me. I hated fighting, it was never a fun desire of mine, but it happened to be the only way to get someone to leave me be. Most of the fights I still don't know what they were for. As I look back at all those young ladies from that time period, some are doing well in life... some are not. I just think of all the energy and emphasis placed on fighting over nothing that could have been put into building each other up.

There are so many broken women in the world and most of it stems from childhood. In middle school I experienced so many challenges within myself and my home. I grew up in a two-parent home until I was around 10 years old, my mom and stepdad finally split up and all the ugly that came from that relationship finally came to an end. Childhood is often Adulthood challenge preparation.

My mom and I didn't see eye to eye as I got older, which I know now is typical of teenagers. She didn't talk to me about boys or how my body would change, I don't think she knew what to say or if my grandmother ever talked to her about those things. With nothing being said I had to figure it out. My answers came from the perverted views of my peers with less knowledge than I had because they were just kids themselves.

As I grew into a teen, I experienced sex at an early age and at just 15 I became pregnant with my first child. Nothing slowed me down while I was pregnant. I still carried on like I had before, but this placed a huge burden on my mom and our relationship. She stuck by me and made sure we had what we needed along with my then boyfriend. I had no clue what I was doing but my mind was so unstable as a 15-year-old I did not know what I was about to experience. I struggled in school; I was reckless with myself because I started not caring about what would happen. I was happy one moment then depressed the next. A baby would soon be my responsibility to care for and train in the way she should go.

When my daughter was born August 1993 a moment in my life stopped and time stood still, she changed my life, her entrance into the world meant that I was now a mom. A single teenage mom still in high school with 3 years left before graduation. What in the world did I get myself into? Once I got into the swing of balancing a kid and school, I began to get my grades back on track and managed to be promoted to the 10<sup>th</sup> grade.

# CHAPTER 2

GOING INTO MY SENIOR YEAR, I FOUND OUT I WAS PREGNANT AGAIN. With this pregnancy I had been in a relationship with the dad a few years. I felt like I would be okay raising this child along with my oldest daughter. I'd matured a little, but I was still a little selfish, still had moments of recklessness in my decision-making.

My second daughter arrived in December of 1995. One of my teachers brought my class work to my home so that I could continue keeping up with school and hopefully graduate with my class June of 1996. Being a parent of two proved to be more than my little finite mind had conceived. The struggle of getting them to daycare and going to school proved to be a beautiful melody of chaos especially with no vehicle of my own. I depended on the mercy of others to help me get to each destination.

I graduated on schedule in June of 1996; I considered joining the military to get away from my little small town, but as a single mom, I would've had to sign my girls over to my mother. I did have enough sense to know that it would be a burden on her to care for two small kids, so I did what everyone else did—I enrolled into community college and got a job. I had the greatest ambitions in my head, I started out going to school for computer science, then nursing, then lab tech, finally becoming a nursing assistant. My plan was to work as an assistant to if see the reality of being a registered nurse was what I really wanted to do in life.

At this point in my life I had gained some stability, I had purchased a car, I had purchased a mobile home, and I was working two jobs and going to school. I also got married July 1999. I was under the preconceived notion that I had a clue of what being a wife was. My husband and I were great together, but we didn't realize the huge sacrifice a marriage takes and that it was more than just saying *I Love You*. I realize it was more me than him that didn't realize the commitment I would have to make to have a lasting relationship. We were only married 11 months and I called it quits.

I was wild and I didn't want to be held down with the responsibility of marriage. I had so much growing up to do. After our split I would go on to have a few less than stellar relationships. I later woke up one day and decided that I was ready to leave my town and move to a city with my new boyfriend. So, I wrote my mom a note and told her I was moving and asked her to take my girls until I got settled. He and I moved to Greensboro NC, I enrolled into community college and majored in medical office administration. I went to school during the day and he was supposed to be working.

A few months into our move I found out that this dude was not working and that we were in danger of not having a place to live. Luckily, I had befriended a lady that graciously let me live with her until we could find another place. That time in my life was so chaotic and getting crazier by the minute. Once I completed my courses, I landed a job at Moses Cone Hospital as a unit clerk. I started to make my own money and I began to also make a plan to leave my boyfriend. I felt if I was going to do bad it would be alone with my kids. God was so gracious in that season of my life I was being kept even in my mess of a life.

I met some amazing people while working at Moses Cone and for the most part I loved my job. I still had dreams of owning a business, owning a home again, being successful, and raising my girls. It would still take me a lot more years to fully begin to understand why I experienced so many hurdles, disappoints, heartbreak, heartache, failures, etc. He had a plan all along of how he would redeem me. If anyone would have told me that God would use me in any capacity, I would have called you a liar and cussed you out. I didn't know that God uses the broken messy places in our life for His good and His glory. I was being redeemed and it all started with a church service back in my hometown. I wasn't crazy about big churches, that was my excuse for not going to church while living in Greensboro along with not feeling worthy enough to be in church due to the life I was living. I had grown up in church.

---

FOR ALMOST FOURTEEN YEARS OUR FAMILY WENT TO THE SAME CHURCH from the time I was a little kid until I became a teenager. I would go home some weekends and that's when I would go to church, mostly to keep from hearing my mothers' mouth about how I should be ashamed of myself not giving God any of my time. So, when I went home to visit, I knew church was a must. Now I did not like being called out for any reason especially in church. I always sat in the back of the church behind someone tall so that my pastor didn't see a need to call me up or out.

That Sunday, something was different, in his message he spoke about Jesus feeding the 5000 with 5 loaves and 2 fish. He demonstrated how Jesus blessed and broke the bread and out of nowhere I heard him call my name, "Dee come on up here," as I walked to the front of my little country church I felt hot all over, in my mind I am thinking he is about to call all my sin out in front of everyone. I had never given my life to Christ, so I just knew I was going to hell in this moment. He said, "Just like Jesus broke the bread in two pieces, so your life is about to split into two crossroads, and you are going to have to make a decision!"

I had no clue what that meant or what decision I was about to make. Up to that moment all my decisions had not been great ones so why would God entrust me to make any decision that would change my life for good or bad. He was setting me up to be uncomfortable when I did make choices that were less than what He had created me to be. My consciousness had been awakened and I would from then on be sensitive to places, activities, thoughts, feelings, words, etc. that had not previously bothered me. God was working on redeeming me.

————

RENEWED

In 2009 I got married and my new husband and I decided to go into the military. After training, our family was stationed at Fort Campbell, KY. In this stage of my life I had added two more kids who were 3 years old and 5 months old. This became a season of pruning in my life. Here I was 600 plus miles away from my family and friends. We had moved before many times; however, this season was new and unlike any move I had journeyed on before. My husband and I had one vehicle so I found myself taking on the role as a stay at home mom with my two youngest daughters. I wasn't happy about being at home all day. I was accustomed to making my own way and being independent. Sometimes I felt isolated and cut off from the world. There would be many disappointments in the days ahead, yet I was challenged with what currently was in front of me another husband and more kids. I had to settle down.

I began to realize that I needed to be a better version of who God created me to be. My mind was made up, even though I felt defeated in how I had raised my older girls I would be a different type of mom to these two girls. I have always said that God gave me what I needed through the personality of my girls. My 3-year-old asked me out of the blue one day why we had not gone to church. Totally mind blowing, out of the mouth of babes was my thought at that moment. I told her that we would find a church so we could start attending. There was a church near our neighborhood right across from the projects. The area looked suspect but I had a desire to be back in church as well. We got dressed one Sunday morning and we went to the church across from the projects. I told my daughter we would start here and see how we felt about it, and if it didn't feel right, we would keep searching.

As we walked into the foyer, we were met with smiles and hugs, which was strange for me. I remember thinking who goes around hugging strangers, never the less they were extremely nice. I was ushered to a seat in the back which was great so I could easily slip out if I wasn't feeling it. As soon as the pastor walked out on the platform my daughter asked why was our pastor from back home here. I felt like it was God's sign that we were in the church that we needed. We began coming to church every Sunday and my heart began to be cultivated and renewed through the Word of God. I had been in church most of my life on and off. But it seemed like this Word was different, colorful and bright, almost like it jumped off the page at me. At some point I started to attend Wednesday nights, then the women's meetings, then small groups. I began to make the best of my time in Clarksville TN, I became involved with many activities within the church and grew through many of them over time.

Then there came a point in my marriage before my husband was deployed that our relationship which was already rocky became even more unstable. During his deployment it got worse. So many ups and downs between us hit such a catastrophic low it seemed impossible for our marriage to work.

After deployment we called it quits and separated. It was ugly at first and for many years after it was bad between us. Everything we experienced we needed it to happen to us, because ultimately it was for us. After the split, my girls and I found ourselves homeless.

We stayed in the friend of friend's basement for a while, then we lived in the living room of a church member. By the time we got into a house of our own we were very grateful for what little we had and for each other. My new challenge was to get everyone where they needed to be. My oldest graduated high school and was looking for a job, my second oldest was completing middle college which meant I had to take her to and from school. I felt defeated on a daily basis, I wanted to give up and move back to NC, but I thought there was nothing there and going back to NC was not going to help me succeed and make a better life for my family. Once we got all moved into the new house, I decided to enroll back into school, I had taken some semesters off since I had so much going wrong in my marriage. I was pursuing my nursing degree because I felt like if I could get this degree I would be in a better financial place to take care of my girls. I needed two more classes to apply to the nursing program.

Those two classes meant I had to drive to Hopkinsville Community College in KY. Luckily, I was able to take all the previous classes at the education center on post at Fort Campbell. The gas to drive to Hopkinsville three times a week was killing me but I was determined to reach this goal for my girls. Early into the semester my car died and I was unable to make the trip to Hopkinsville for class, so I had to withdraw.

This was a devastation blow to my confidence and my plan. I know God knew this would happen, He was carrying me through this time of transition and uncertainty. During the time I was going to school I worked part time at The UPS Store. Now without school I went back full time and threw myself into learning all I could about UPS. I grew out of my comfort zone working with people and the public which was challenging. I hated confrontation so the idea of a customer becoming irate because of service terrified me at first, however I learned how to handle conflict and keep my customers happy.

The job took a lot of my time, sometimes working a 10-hour days lifting, packing, and shipping that became my norm. I enjoyed it so much over the years until I had a desire in my heart to own a UPS Store one day. As I grew my relationship with God, he also placed a woman in my life to help guide and usher me into a new season of growth, accountability, and stripping away of preconceived notions about who God was, is, and could be in my life. She became a very valuable resource in my growth and development. I have to say that she cultivated a love for God's ways in my life, she pushed and encouraged me to grow through adversity and trials, to focus on helping another person as she did for me, to give God all my worries and cares. She and her husband were the ones that helped us get the house we moved into. She was my role model and mentor. I remember when I asked her to mentor me, she responded, "You want me? I am jacked up!"

At that time, I was pretty messed up myself so she was exactly what I needed. This renewal process God had me on changed me from the outside/in, which probably doesn't make sense but that's how he did me. I changed how I looked on the outside, no jewelry, jeans and pants, no makeup. This is how I had lived my life for over 5 years, this is how all the women around me looked. I learned that God didn't care about what I looked like on the outside if I had changed what was on the inside. My heart... my heart was what God was after. He needed me to become the woman of influence he created because I would be given an assignment later and I needed to be fit spiritually and mentally to accomplish His purpose, I was being renewed.

––––––

RESTORED

What a year 2016 was so many good things happened that year, as well as a few tragedies. My sister got married, a close friend was diagnosed with cancer, my father passed away, and I was demoted on my job.

Three years later it's more of a blur, but I remember bits and pieces in detail. My father's passing was life altering. I was in deep turmoil and I felt so bad for my mom and sister because he was everything to them. I had only been around this side of my family a few years, so the fact that I felt like I didn't get enough time with him made for a very bitter person within. I had wasted so much time not really living in the moment with my family. I can still remember the hugs from my father as I got closer to him. This made me miss him even more after he passed. I felt empty, guilty and resentful since I still hadn't resolved my anger with my dad due to his absence in my life growing up. I felt like my life would have been much different if I had him there growing up. Now he was gone and I don't think I ever shared with him how even as an adult I felt like a kid around him.

My father's death helped me to see and understand how important family really is. I began to really reflect on whether or not my life was really making a difference in anyone's life. I realized in that moment that I was not living life to its fullest. My life was simply just full of habit and routine. I came back to Tennessee from the funeral to total chaos in my mind. Asking myself what was next. Initially I went back to the routine of my life but I was so restless. I felt like the Holy Spirit had given me an instruction, but I was too afraid to take it. The instruction was it's time for you to resign from your job. I asked the Holy Spirit how would I take care of my family if I resigned from my job.

The only response I got was a month and a day, February 27th, to resign from my job. I scheduled an appointment to speak with my Pastor, he asked me a series of questions about what I did, what would I like to do, what would I do if I didn't have this job. I honestly didn't have an answer because I never planned on leaving the UPS Store, I was going to be a store owner one day. How was I supposed to know what would I do if I had to do something else?

I left his office feeling better from the recommendation he gave me. Which was to pray about it some more so I could have a plan for the shifting between jobs. So early July 2017 I heard the voice of God again telling me it was time for me to leave The UPS Store. I was genuinely reluctant to make such a bold move with no other income coming into the house. what was I going to do to take care of my family? I had planned a trip to North Carolina to visit family right before the kids went back to school. I was so afraid to resign from my career, but I had to trust that God was in control and that my obedience could lead to something greater. I didn't share with anyone when I put my notice in or when I left. My then supervisor was shocked when I handed her my letter of resignation, she told me she wouldn't turn it in until after I had returned in case I changed my mind while I was gone. I knew if I was trusting God I could not change my mind because it wasn't my mind to change. I visited my family and returned to Clarksville, when I pulled in the driveway I said, "Ok Holy Spirit what now?" I was challenged by God to "be still and know" that is all I got from Him.

My nerves were a wreck most of the time I worried, stressed, cried, and called out to God. I honestly can't say one specific way the bills got paid but they did and nothing was turned off, my landlord didn't put me out because of late rent, and we ate. Only God could have sustained me in these moments, his hand was upon me in these moments of uncertainty, of feeling like a failure or that I heard wrong. I kept repeating scriptures to my thoughts, it was the scriptures that kept me pushing and moving forward.

I started attending The Tabernacle Church late November 2016, and every message at that time seemed to be meeting me right where my thinking had been during the week. I loved the church, its culture and its diversity. I eventually attended membership class and started serving within the church.

This was new but it felt right. I began to discover what a relationship with God really looked like. This teaching was more about transforming me from the inside out. I was encouraged each Sunday and I had the worship and the message stored into my heart. I was being restored, I was learning that my past was just that...my past and that Jesus didn't even remember the things I had done. I was a brand-new creature in Christ.

I was serving in The TAB Café one morning and one of the pastors came up and asked me how I was doing and my reply was, "Getting use to not working." I had not planned on sharing this fact with him, but I am glad I did.

I was trying to be still but, it was a challenge so while I was waiting for God to show me my next step, I applied for The UPS hub. The job was not what I wanted but I needed to fix my situation. I went for an interview and the gentlemen interviewing me said, "Ms. Tyler are you sure this is what you want to do?"

My response was a solid no, but I needed the job to take care of my family.

He then said, "Would you like to apply for a position like what I do?"

This idea excited me. I left feeling accomplished and noticed for my managerial skills. I I went home told my daughter, her BFF and her boyfriend about the opportunity and that they should apply. God then just kicked me in the face because all three of them applied, got hired and started working, all before I ever got a second interview.

I was shaking my head asking God why? In another week I got a phone call for a second interview. While waiting on the interview with UPS, one of the pastors from our congregation recommended that I apply for an upcoming position within the church that was becoming available soon. He told me to go online and apply. I was very hopeful for the church position because it was closer to home than driving to Nashville every day. I went to the second interview with UPS and was asked the same question.

"Do you really want to apply for this job?"

This time I said yes. At the end of my interview I was told I would meet with one more person. The interview was scheduled for a Wednesday.

I was super excited.

The church also interviewed me the same week I had the interview with UPS. I had a great feeling about The TAB position the interview had been perfect. So now I was waiting for a response.

I interviewed at UPS a third time and the lady asked me, "Are you sure this is what you want to do?"

I was screaming inside my head. By now I was tired of responding to that question. I need a job I responded to her and I know UPS so I feel like this is a perfect fit for me. She sat and looked at me, she asked me some more interview questions and when we wrapped that up, she informed me that I would receive a call or email regarding their decision for the position on Friday.

Can I tell you God has such a strange sense of humor? I received an offer letter from The TAB on that Thursday! I was extremely excited at how God's fingerprint was all over this. I had been stressing and trying to make things happen within my own strength, not realizing that God had a plan all along.

When UPS called on Friday, I was happy to inform them that another offer had been extended and I would not be accepting the position with them. I think God used each of those interviewers to stall me, so that the glory of God could be shown in the transition of my life. Coming into The TAB was the fruit of showing me that I had been restored to share His gospel, His glory, and His hand in my life. I have grown so much on my journey with The TAB. I have been in the kitchen of The TAB for almost 2 years and to see people partake of the fruits that are labored out during the week is breathtaking. I was redeemed, renewed, and restored to be a light in dark places for others, to be a key to unlock someone else's prison, to be a word of encouragement and hope to others. My life is not my own as the word says, the ministry within me has the opportunity to be used by God for the up building of His kingdom so that none will be lost. If I can be redeemed, renewed, and restored…anyone can.

# AUTHOR BIO: DETRA TYLER

Detra Tyler can usually be found reading a influentially positive and thought provoking book. Sharing her story of impact moments was her thrust from God, which will help women overcome their past and share their story.

Detra enjoys spending time with family and friends creating memories and learning to be in the present moment. Her passion is to be a relevant voice to single moms, sharing her ups and downs to encourage them in their faith, and hopefully provide words of wisdom, a hug of comfort and an ear to listen along the way.

She is the mother of four beautiful daughters Tasia, Khadijah, Olivia and Isabella. At the cusp of becoming the ever-evolving woman God created her to be, Detra is hub of The Tabernacle Church as Administrator Director. Serving her community through outreach, connect groups and serving in her local church. Detra is a native of Chadbourn NC.

# IN SPITE OF ME

## Iretha Alston

# CHAPTER 1

## The Beginning of the End

BEFORE I WRITE ABOUT MY TEST, WHICH TURNED INTO MY TESTIMONY, I would like to thank the visionary Tonya Joyner Scott for her obedience in listening to God. Thank you for Project Shine.

To the readers, I pray that my truth will bless you in ways you never thought. I give all thanks to my Mom who instilled Christ in me at very young age.

The growing lump in my breast ignited a feeling of impending doom. I lay in bed mid-March doing a breast exam as I have done for the past 15 years. Only to find a large lump.

I made an appointment to see the doctor on the 19th of April which also happened to be the birthday of my oldest child. As I waited in the lobby, my mind was overrun with questions: *Will I get to see my only grandchild grow up? What will I tell my family? Will they support me?* Deep down, I was terrified of what my doctor was going to tell me. I was immediately scheduled for surgery on May 1st. I felt a whirlwind of emotions and felt inadequate to keep up—my world was spinning so fast.

The week before surgery, my best friend had a massive stroke. I had just been with her the previous November. My heart felt like it had left my body because our last parting had ended on a sour note.

However, her son reached out to me which gave me a little comfort. Her funeral was scheduled for the following Friday before my surgery. It was my intent to fly to New York on that morning and return later that evening. Her son called me back and persuaded me to stay home and focus on my own health.

It was confirmed that I had breast cancer on a Monday morning, and would need another surgery to remove the rest of the cancer. My first thought was *not me*. I did my yearly breast exams—sometimes twice a year. How could this happen to me? After the doctors took a closer look, it was determined that the right breast had to be removed. On June 14th, 2019 they did a myectomy.

———

ONLY IN MY MOTHER'S DEATH DID I REALIZE HOW MUCH SHE LOVED me. I was born in Spring Hope, North Carolina. My mother moved to Newark, New Jersey when I was a baby, and this is where I grew up. She was a single mom of seven; I was her sixth child. We had very little but in my eyes, she was super mom because she managed to take care of all of us by herself.

My mom sent us to North Carolina every summer to stay with my grandparents, so we could crop tobacco and pick cucumbers to get our school clothes for the next year. I used to hate going in the fields especially the cucumber fields it was hot and all you could see from one end of the field to the other was cucumbers. I would sweat like a puppy. There was about 10-12 of us living in a three-bedroom house with outdoor pluming and no running water. Taking a bath in wash tub was the most humiliating thing I ever knew. We had to pour water into a pump and then boil it on a wood heater.

I remember the summer when the abuse began. I woke up with my bottom wet or Vaseline in my back side. I had no real understanding of what was going on. Once I realized what it was, I never thought to tell anyone, and it became the norm for me. I thought that's what relatives were supposed to do to 6-year-old little girls. This went on every summer until I was 10.

When my mom decided to return to North Carolina to live, I was horrified. Although I didn't fully understand what was happening—I felt the deep sense of shame and knew instinctively that it didn't feel right. Even being an adult now I remember the feeling of shame and guilt that would come over me when I would be in the room with the member of my family that I know now was having sex with me.

Nevertheless, we moved to North Carolina some of us had to stay with my grandmother. I was with my mom and thought I was free from all the bad things. However, one of my older brothers started molesting me and even tried to brainwash me into thinking that it was normal. He got married at age 16, and every time I lay eyes on him, I thought about how he molested me just 3 years earlier. I wouldn't share this with anyone what had been happening, but I hated him.

———

YEARS LATER, THAT SAME BROTHER ENDED UP IN PRISON AND WHILE there, he became very sick. My mother called to say that it didn't look good and we should go see him. "*Let him die,*" was my response to her. He had caused a lot of pain and hurt not only for me but also to others. God intervened that night and laid on my heart that despite everything —this man was still my brother. He reminded me that to have grace is to show grace.

I went to visit him in Butner Prison that following Monday. I walked into the room looking at what use to be a strong man who now looked like he was in his 90's. His hair was gone and all I could do was stare with a heavy heart unable at the time to tell him that all was forgiven.

A few years later while in therapy, I wrote him a letter telling him what he had done to me and how it made me feel. I didn't send it though—I tore it up and let it go. Once I did that, I asked God to forgive me and that I had forgiven him.

My brother passed away that same day.

I had peace with his passing, but I also had pain. Carrying the burden of all the things that had happened to me as a child, I went into my late teens never dating or learning how to identify healthy relationships. I was madly in love at this time with a guy who was one grade higher than myself his name was James. I was friends with his sibling John, who despite him telling me his brother didn't care for me, I gave James my virginity, after which he stopped talking to me. I was 17 at the time.

John and I became close throughout high school. The day before I left to go to basic training, I had sex with John. I never thought twice about it, even though I felt it was wrong and deep down I was really still in love with James. But it was John who seemed to really care about me, so we began dating seriously.

# CHAPTER 2

## A God of Many Chances

I joined the National Guard and was stationed at Ft. Jackson SC. It was one of the most challenging times of my life, but I made it through. Once I got to Active Individual Training (AIT), at Fort Benjamin Harrison in Indiana. I was there for about two weeks when I was called out of formation by the first sergeant who was over our battalion and he took me to his room and told me that I would do what he said, or he would end my career. I was only 18 years old and all I wanted to do was make my mother proud. Depression set in because I didn't care what I had to do—I was not willing to go home a failure.

During that time, to go to someone higher in command would have just ended my career. I couldn't tell anyone what I was going through and had to lie about what I was doing. I had begun to think I was in a relationship with this Sargent, because except for the sexual abuse, he really didn't treat me bad. However, one day he took me to a hotel instead of sneaking me in his room. He brought a friend and allowed him to do what he wanted to me. I remember that day going into the hospital for a migraine. The pain was so bad that I thought all my organs were coming out of my body. They kept me overnight.

My drinking increased in an effort to cope with all I had to endure and the childhood trauma I'd experienced. Once my time ended to leave, I was so grateful. I never wanted to see that Sargent again.

Upon my return, I went to my assigned unit. The Staff Sergeant I met before I left for Basic Training pulled me into her office one afternoon, "What's going on with you? You're not the same spunky girl I met."

I broke down and shared what I'd been through. She advised me to get help. I refused. I assured her I was fine.

I was never so wrong.

I was very rebellious in nature... a fighter. After a stint in a Civil Service job, I returned to active duty. I was drinking heavily, but a good employee. Around this time, John and I had been dating for a couple of years. We decided to get married. Things were good but not great.

One of my soldiers introduced me to Cocaine and it made me believe I could do my job much better. It gave me that feeling of being on top of the world. I could move faster and answer any question asked. It made me feel like I had superpowers. I had no idea at the time that it was the beginning of an even bigger down fall.

One day while shopping with my cousin, we stopped at the shop where my husband was helping someone. Afterward, he called me on the side of the building where I first experienced crack cocaine.

I hated it. It made me feel sick.

At some point, I was at a card game, drinking and snorting power all night. My husband was already gone but I. I remember calling to say that I was hurting really bad in my stomach. He came and took me to the hospital.

We found out that I was pregnant, and it was in my tubes, so they had to do a DNC. Apparently, the doctor who'd told me I couldn't have children—didn't know what he was talking about. I was told to wait at least six months before trying to have another child. I felt an insurmountable joy at discovering I would be able to have children.

Seven months later, I became pregnant again. We found that my husband had sickle cell anemia which ignited countless days and nights in and out of the hospital on top of his drugs addiction. The doctor took me out of work and off my feet when I was three months pregnant. I had completely stopped drinking and using drugs during my pregnancy. Life was pretty good during this time.

———

EIGHT WEEKS AFTER I HAD MY SON, IT WAS TIME TO GO BACK TO WORK. I had to do more training at Fort Benjamin Harrison. I kissed my son and my husband and off I went. Four days later I enter the bowling alley, only to see my former abuser. I was petrified. He was an MSG over my battalion. This is not what I wanted my life. I had a son and a husband. I just wanted to be left alone.

The first words out of his mouth were how he'd missed me.

I was in for another round of hell. I attempted to fight back this time. I even when to the Commander of the post office and got scared to knock. I even thought about killing myself and just being done. I begin drinking again and this time it was more than I can even measure.

# CHAPTER 3

## The Only Free Thing in Life is Salvation

I RETURNED HOME AND BEGIN USING COCAINE AGAIN. MY HUSBAND and I got high together—we were functional addicts. I was getting all the cocaine I wanted for free from my soldiers in exchange for completing their paperwork. My husband persuaded me to try crack again. After everything life had thrown at me—it became my best friend.

Despite abusing drugs, we were still able to manage our home. I was making good money and he was a stay-at-home dad. Life was good. My husband was still sick—there were frequent hospital visits and times when I had to find someone to care for my son during the day. On top of this, I was diagnosed with Hepatitis C and ended up in the hospital for seven days. When I was released from the hospital, I took the baby and went to my mother's house to recuperate.

Three days later, I felt better and wanted to get my hair cut. I was approached by some man from a nearby bar who proceeded to tell me that he had nine returned checks that I'd written. I immediately checked all my accounts, only to find out my husband and my brother had spent over $10,000 dollars.

I was broke.

I called my husband and of course he had no clue—at least this is what he wanted me to believe. I left him and moved in with my mother, but for only a short time. My son stayed with her full time, but I went to live with my youngest sibling.

I started using more and more. My life was all about my drugs. Nothing else mattered.

The sister I was living with met someone and moved away. I followed her and started sleeping with her drug dealing boyfriend. She didn't know. After they broke up, I spent the night with him.

She and my older sister walked in and beat the snot out of me. I tried to take my life after that by slitting my wrist and refusing to go to the hospital that night. However, I went the next day and was committed to a mental institution for seven days.

I eventually returned to work, but my job performance dropped as I was still using drugs. A week later, I walked into my boss's office and I told him I had a problem. He opened his desk drawer and requested I take a drug test. I was busted down one rank, but he allowed me to go to treatment.

I went to Macon Georgia for over six months only to come home and remain clean for about three months. I had gone to the doctor by this time and was given a diagnosis of Bipolar 1, which went untreated, so I started abusing drugs again, and stopped going to work altogether.

My boss called me one day and demanded that I send in my ID card. I did as he asked and was given an Honorable Discharge. I now realize this was God. He could have marked me AWOL for not showing up.

# CHAPTER 4

## The Cost

THE COST

My love affair with drugs continued, but there is always a cost.

My car was repossessed. I lost my home and had to move back in with the sister I'd done so wrong. I met a wonderful man but did not fully appreciate him the way I should. Thankfully, he remains one of best friends. I went to rehab after rehab, but it was to please others—it was never for me. This guy and I moved to Virginia hoping this would slow me down, but to no avail—I found my drugs there, too.

We eventually returned to North Carolina. I cheated on him and got pregnant. We both knew the baby wasn't his, but we decided not to disclose that the baby wasn't his. I stopped using during the pregnancy and for several years after. When he asked me to marry him, I panicked and looked for a way out, so I began abusing drugs again.

It worked because he left me.

I wanted to keep using so I told him to come get his child and he did. During this time, my oldest son was living with me, having been with my mother for most of his life. The continuous rhythm of getting treatment for everyone else but me continued. I lost everything I had three times during this 10-year cycle. The consequences of this is that my son was beginning to do the same things I was doing and despite how strung out I was at the time—I was not having that.

We got into an argument one day and he raised his hand to hit me. I knew I had to do something before this got out of control. So, I called my brother who lived in Alaska and asked if he would take him. He sent the ticket immediately. I have nothing but gratitude and grace for the two men who raised my children when I couldn't.

My son was not only my son—he was also the only friend I had. For about two weeks after he left, I cried myself to sleep. I only found peace in my drug-induced euphoria. It had gotten so bad that I was stealing and doing things that I am not proud of. I clearly recall a time when I was getting high with some so-called friends and we began a conversation about the Bible. I can't remember what the topic was about, but I asked him to let me see his. When he said he didn't have one, I knew it was time for me to get out of that house. I may have strayed, but my mom brought me up in church and I would not be in a place where the Word was not present.

My life continued to spiral downward. I became a drug mule. I did this for several years. There are always consequences for the decisions we make. One memorable moment is the day I was arrested and charged with eight felonies. I'd gone to get a haircut. I'd been drinking and was driving a car with drugs inside and fake tags.

As I pulled into the barber shop, the police drove in behind me. They searched the car but initially did not find anything. I'd hidden the crack under the seat. They brought a female cop to inspect the car and she found it. I was taken to the station and charged. A drug dealing friend of mine paid half of my bail and my son's father paid the other half.

I was once again homeless and had to move in with my niece. Not long after, I attended a party with that same friend. While there, I had a conversation with his wife who invited me to attend church with her on Sunday. I accepted her invitation with no real expectations of anything.

When Sunday came around, I got up and did what I'd always done —got high. When it was close to time for service to start, she called and said she was sending someone to pick me up. I quickly got dressed and met her there. What I saw that day would change my life forever. This was a defining moment in my life.

Let me preface what I'm about to tell you by mentioning that there was this one guy I dated who I'd visit, and his "sister" would answer the door. I later found out that she was his *wife*. I think back to how my life could have ended right there...

*But God.*

On this particular Sunday, I saw that same woman. She had remarried with four children who clearly adored her. She was the image of a Proverbs 31 woman and I knew deep down that God had blessed her for her faithfulness. Tears ran down my face as I acknowledged the contrast of our lives.

Later that evening, the woman who'd invited me to church told me that she had an uncle in Philadelphia who could help me if I really wanted to get clean. She gave me his number.

I didn't use it. I was on a path of destruction and while this was not the life I wanted; I didn't know how to stray from the course. I was stealing, sleeping around, and doing what I could do to ignore my tumultuous feelings. I used drugs to live and lived to use drugs.

On Sunday, the 27th of July in 2008, I started the day drinking and cutting a fool. One moment of introspection and it hit me: I was sick and tired of being sick and tired.

I broke the bottle I'd been drinking from and began to cry out, "God take me or take this away from me. Thank God for his sovereignty."

I was delivered instantly, but I knew I needed to get away. The next thing I did was call the number I'd been given.

There was no answer.

I called my friend and she told me she'd try to reach her uncle and she'd call me right back.

The next time my phone rang, and I answered, the voice on the other side said, "You don't ever have to use anything again."

# CHAPTER 5

## A New Beginning

I TALKED WITH THE YOUNG LADY FOR ABOUT TWENTY MINUTES AND SHE gave me some resources I could use to get treatment I needed. The first place I called was "Fresh Start" and the only way to get into their recovery house was to interview in person, which meant I had to go to Philadelphia.

I was getting a check on Monday but the bus left Sunday night, so I had to borrow enough money for my one-way ticket and a carton of cigarettes. When I arrived, I was told by a woman there that she couldn't let me in that house, but she had another one down the street where she gave me a bed. I laid in my top bunk that night I can't explain the feelings that were taking me over and the song came on the radio, Let Go and Let God. That's what I did.

I had a court date at the end of September for the charges I mentioned earlier. I was charged with a misdemeanor possession of crack cocaine. All the other charges had been dropped. However, when I sat down with my attorney, I was informed that the actual charge was felony possession of crack cocaine. I told my lawyer I would not plead guilty to that because I had people in the system, and I wouldn't be able to visit them. He informed me that it was going to take some time and I would have to be in court every month. Disappointed, and only one and half months clean I couldn't return to the "Fresh Start" program.

I had no idea how I was going to stay clean but I remembered the first couple of things I learned early on: "To thine self be true," and "Go to the same lengths to stay clean as I did to get high."

That's what I did. I started going to NA meetings on a regular basis and sometimes I had to walk two or three miles to get there.

When I got my court date, the judge gave me 60 day suspended sentence with 24 months supervised probation.

*This was amazing.*

The man I was sleeping with convinced me that I could do the 60 days and then we could go on with our life. He promised to visit me, and we made plans for our future. I took his advice and went to my probation officer with two months of payments. It had been about thirty days and she told me to take my money back. Three weeks later she violated me for non-payment.

When I went before the judge, I opted to do the time instead of paying the $90 I owed. My son had given me a Bible. I figured I could take it with me to help pass the time.

I was good until they took my Bible because it was a hardcover book. I couldn't stop the tears.

*Lord what am I going to do?*

I asked the bailiff if I could please make one call before they locked me up. I called my mom; gave her the name of that Bible and then asked her to mail the paperback version.

I did 45 days in county jail. I saw more in lock-up than was going on in real life. Sex, drugs, you name it; it was happening. The guy I'd been seeing didn't visit me once or accept any of my calls. It hurt because I was in love with him. I later found out he was also dating a young lady who happened to be a friend of mine. I guess that's why he wanted me to take the jail time.

# CHAPTER 6

## A Wayward Child

AFTER I WAS RELEASED FROM JAIL, I DECIDED TO GO BACK TO school. I wanted to make some positive changes in my life. However, in the middle of the second year I was diagnosed with Stage 4 liver cancer. God kept me through this trial, and I am forever grateful.

I had been clean for a year when I met who I thought was the most amazing man in the world and although we didn't believe in the same God—I was in love with him. I begin searching for a church family—I started doing ministry and my life seemed full, until one day my ministry leader told me that we had to volunteer in the Outreach center four hours a week—which also happened to be led by my son's step-mother. I really thought nothing of it. I called and set my hours up and I was so excited.

The day before I was supposed to start serving, I was laying on my mother's bed when my phone rang. The voice on the other side of the phone was a lady and she said, "You can't serve in this ministry because you and the ministry leader have history, if you don't like it you can take it up with the pastor."

The call ended with a click, then the line went dead.

I began to cry and ask God why. I fell asleep and had a dream where God said, "I never gave up on you, so why are you giving up on me?"

I felt so bad that everyone else was doing the hours and I couldn't I stepped down from that ministry and joined the drama team and the transportation ministry, never giving up on God because he didn't give up on me.

I sat under this leadership for over five years. During that time, I had several church hurts that all involved my son's stepmother. This was a woman in training to be a minister. I thought if this is being a real Christian than I don't want any part of this. I remember one time going in the sanctuary and trying to hug her and she turned her back on me with another minister present. I sent her an email asking her to forgive me for anything I had done. To no avail. God forgave me and I forgave myself.

––––––––

MY MOM PASSED AWAY.

Two weeks later, I picked up my son— the one who's stepmother wouldn't do anything for him. They attended the same church, but he couldn't ride with her. I pulled up to get him and my son's stepmother walked up to my window and began screaming about her husband. I reminded her that I gave him to her.

By this time, my son's is getting out of the car and says, "Mrs.---- go in the house. This is not worth it."

She puts her hand in my son's face. I got out of my car saying, "If you ever put your hands on my child again, I will beat your a\*\*."

She pushed me and it took all of her neighbors to get me off her. I took my anger over losing my mother and being denied a place in the ministry outreach on her. At the time, it was worth it to me, but before I could get home, she had taken a warrant out on me.

My son was angry with me. I will never forget his words. "Look at y'all out here calling yourselves women of God. You go to the same church and out here fighting. Shame on both of you. I was looking for a sit down with the pastor for sure. Or at least a conversation about what had happened and why."

It never came.

We went to court and the charges were dropped because my lawyer spoke with her neighbors and they stated that she had started the fight. She had also taken a restraining order against me.

The pastor took my son under his wing and began training him to be a minister/leader. I remember sitting in the congregation listening to my son as he preached. Afterward, the pastor asked for the parents of my child to stand. This so-called Christian woman stood up when she couldn't care less for my son. I wanted to take off my shoe and throw it at her. Thank God for change.

After 17 years of being on total disability, I secured a job working with Veteran Affairs where I made more money than I had ever made in my life. I moved from the city I was into another city closer to my job and purchased my first home and a brand-new car. For the first time in years, I had something in my name. God repaired my credit.

———

A YEAR LATER, I WAS ABLE TO PURCHASE MY SECOND HOME.

The man I loved—the one I thought was everything I could want in a companion… in reality, it was nothing more than a sex-a-ship—never the relationship I desired. I had given this guy the best eight years of my life. I still had low self-esteem and thought I was unlovable by anyone else. I allowed this guy to move another woman in his house only to start hanging out at mines because he didn't know how to put her out. He was out of work for a whole year, and I did everything I could for him. I even wired him money to go hang with the fellows.

We got back together, and I stayed with him until I was tired of dealing with the cheating, lies, and no love at all. He got married eight months after we broke up, but before he got married, we started talking again. At that time, I had no idea he was getting married, but it had to be God who told him to tell me the truth. He told me that following Friday.

I was hurt, angry, and other emotions I can't really put into words. Marriage is serious and a covenant with God. I told him I couldn't understand why he was messing up that girl's life but with a wife, there was no room in his life for me. I made a decision that day that I would not settle for anything less than what God wanted me to have. If God wanted me to engage in sexual activities ever again, he would send my husband to find me.

I was still in love with him despite everything. I eventually learned that he didn't know how to love because he didn't know God. I once inquired as to what he wanted in a woman, to which he responded, "One with no voice."

This definitely wasn't me.

I tried to be his friend, but I saw so much more in him than he saw in his self to the point that I had to walk away—this time for good. I continued praying for God to cover this man.

I kept my promise to remain celibate. I had to pray daily to stay on this path. I never gave up on the vision God gave me when he delivered me from drugs and alcohol in 2008. I was given the assignment to plant ministries all over the world.

I went to Texas to visit my family and attended a church who had a similar ministry. I asked that leader how I could adapt it to start my own. She shared that I would have to complete the training at the founding church. I took that training. I knew deep down that all I had to do was trust God. He is faithful.

After I completed my training, there came a point when I was asked to be a speaker at an event in Philadelphia. While there, I met a pastor who was from the town where I grew up. We had a brief discussion over lunch, then went our separate ways. I had been dealing with some health struggles along with issues on the job for the past two or three years. On the way home from Philadelphia, I clearly heard God say, "Time Freedom."

I remember saying, "God, I can't quit my job."

I went to bed one night and woke up hearing, *ram in the bush; time freedom, and leave the job.* I have to say that we serve an on-time God. I went to my doctor and asked him to take me out of work. He did as I requested under FMLA. God had laid it on my heart to request a medical-retirement due to all the stress and anxiety the job was causing. God granted me the early retirement.

I began helping Veterans complete medical claims, and anything I could do to serve others. At this time, I wasn't fully aware of what God was preparing me for, but I trusted Him. I'd left the church I was attending and started watching different church services online. I gave my tithes to various organizations. I still had no clear picture of what God wanted me to do and at this point, I was tired of attending churches where the people weren't following God but following man.

# CHAPTER 7

## Be Careful and Know He's God

ONE DAY, I WAS RIDING DOWN HIGHWAY 64 WHEN I GOT A TEXT THAT read:

*I am doing the final inspections on my building would love to sit down and talk about that ministry if you're still interested.*

I got so excited I pulled off the highway and did a Facebook live and titled it, when you think God has forgotten you. I met with a pastor later that day, and we decided I would be a part of her vision. I started serving with them and became one of her leaders. I watched as she supported other ministries but when it came time to start mine, she never showed up for the meeting, however it had gone well in her absence. She was doing great things in the city, but I began to feel that it wasn't about the people—it was cultivating donors for her non-profit organization.

I felt left out. I couldn't get a call or text back whenever I reached out to her, so I stepped down to avoid sowing discord among the leadership team. It was not what God had shown me in my vision.

I recognized that I'd made it through my battles because God had me from the beginning, I've had lots of professional help and spiritual guidance. I have been hospitalized more than 25 times for mental health or drug addiction reasons. I celebrated 11 years of deliverance from substance abuse July 2019 and have been free of all types of medication for the past three years. This is because I completely surrendered to God. I thank God every day of my life that I don't look like what I been through. I can say I have been in the fire, but I don't smell like smoke.

# CHAPTER 8

## Today is a New Day

I AM NOW IN STAGE THREE BREAST CANCER AND CURRENTLY undergoing chemo and radiation treatment. Some may ask, "Aren't you battle weary?"

No, because I've surrendered this situation to the Lord—I trust and leave Him to fight this battle. I know God has no microwave's answers for me He currently has me in the crock pot and all I can do is look to the hills from which cometh my strength.

God has seen me through many dark moments in my life. He has seen me at my worse, but not once did he allow death to take me. He is a patient God; allowing me to make my mistakes and do exactly as I wanted, yet his love for me never waned. He welcomed me with open arms when his prodigal daughter decided to come home. I am surrounded by His love and his peace warms me. I know that through every storm we encounter in this life—a blessing follows.

I pray that you find a measure of comfort in this telling of my truth. Keep your heart and mind stayed on Christ Jesus and there is no end to where you can go or what you can overcome.

*Train a child in the way he should go, and when he is old, he will not depart from it.*

Proverb 22:6 NKJV

This is my favorite Bible verse, because I went down all the wrong paths in my life, but it was my mother's training me about my Heavenly Father, His unconditional love, and His promises. When I was ready, I returned to Him and it was only then that I was made whole.

I want to leave you with these words: today is a new day—a chance to write a new chapter. No matter how far you may have strayed in the past; each day you wake up is another opportunity to get back on track. Another day to get it right. Another day to walk into the arms of your loving Father and be washed clean of your past. You can be made clean, in spite of yourself—it's called Grace....

# AUTHOR BIO: IRETHA ALSTON

Iretha Alston was born in Spring Hope NC and raised in Newark New Jersey. She studied Christian Ministry at Liberty University and is a 9 year Veteran of the United States Army.

Iretha is the proud mother of two children and one stepson along with two beautiful grandsons. A woman who believes in God, Iretha uses her experiences in life to help others transform their circumstances into a success story.

As a Peer Support Specialist, Iretha has served Veterans at the VA Hospital for over 5 years. She continues to provide support services and assistance to the community.

Follow Iretha on Instagram: @irethaalston
Contact information: Irethaa@hotmail.com

# THE WALLS WITHIN

## Nettie Williams

# CHAPTER 1

I NEVER KNEW THE PAIN I ENCOUNTERED, WOULD CAUSE ME TO TAKE someone's life. It started around the summer of 1977. It was hot, no wind stirring at all. But it didn't matter to me, being outdoors was what I loved more than the air I breathed. I loved nature, found joy in walking through narrow paths, leading to the trough where my dad raised hogs. The stench didn't matter. I always felt a sense of independence when walking this path.

During my walks, I would dream and dream big. I wanted to be successful, play basketball in the WNBA. I wanted to pave the way for others, giving them hope, when it seemed all hope was gone. This passion would grow so deep, nothing could wipe it out of my mind. I felt as if I was born with a basketball in my hand. I loved basketball. I would turn down a meal just to be able to stay outside and play. There wasn't a day that passed that I didn't pick up that ball, either in school or at home.

Would this be the turning point for me and my Mom? Would this be the opportunity I waited for? I poured my heart and soul into becoming one of the best basketball players ever. Although there were many accomplishments, nothing seem to could heal the pain I carried in my heart.

# CHAPTER 2

MY INNOCENCE WAS STOLEN FROM ME, DEPRIVING ME OF WHAT COULD have been so many precious moments. Things I'd heard my father say over the years: fast in the behind... trying to be grown... stuff that often made me wonder if I'd done something to warrant those words. Was it the way I walked or carried myself? Had my father been right in his assessment of me—this was perhaps my worst fear.

When it was over, I headed home and pretended nothing happened. I was too ashamed, and I wasn't strong enough to bear my father's wrath, which I felt would surely come. The pain went so deep, that had I not buried it; I would still be holding onto unforgiveness.

My focus shifted from basketball. All I wanted to do was bury my face never to be seen again. The little girl, who once believed she could accomplish whatever task at hand, was now lost in the shuffle. I built a wall around me. I only wanted to make my parents proud of me—to show myself worthy of their love. But all I ended up doing was placing myself in a position to be violated. My dreams eroded as I struggled to understand why my life was filled with nights sobbing and suffering in silence.

My young life was challenging and affected my self-confidence and state of being happy. On the outside, I looked like I had it all together, but I was a mess on the inside. I hid my pain beneath a smile and my laughter.

I eventually buried myself in a part-time job and basketball. I had become somewhat of an expert at wearing a mask. Nobody ever really knew that my life was in shambles. I couldn't let the deep emotional wounds from what had happened to me show. It was my secret shame.

I spent a lot of time throughout my high school years seeking the approval of my parents which later transitioned to my becoming a people pleaser. I continued to work on my basketball skills, but to be honest—I just never felt good enough. Would this horrible feeling ever go away? Would I ever feel whole again?

I'd allowed the man who violated me to make me a victim—one who felt responsible for what had happened to me. I blamed myself for everything that took place, all the bad stuff. I questioned my parent's love for me. From my young perspective, I felt rejected, especially by my father. This belief carried over into my adult life. If my own father didn't love me—how could I expect anyone else to love me? Although there were times, I felt he was proud of me especially when I played well and scored high, but my dad would never say it. He made my first basketball goal, from a bicycle rim nailed to the tree. My dad would play with me and my brothers—he taught us the basics of the game.

I couldn't understand why he didn't love me or why he never saw or said anything good about me. My mom wasn't an affectionate woman—she and my father shared that in common, but I felt closer to her. I yearned for a relationship with my dad. I was too young to understand that people show love in various capacities. People have different love languages and one of mine is affirmations and compliments. I craved this from my parents.

Although my father barely had a kind word for me—he never missed one of my games. How I wished he could've given me a hug or just the utterance of *I love you* from time to time. It's what my heart wanted to hear most.

The wall erected around my heart had become a permanent fixture.

———

WHEN THE ONLY COACH IN HIGH SCHOOL I KNEW SWITCHED FROM coaching the girls to varsity boys. I felt abandoned once again. It's all so familiar now, it was starting to feel like the norm.

However, I never once considered quitting basketball. I loved the sport too much.

I was recruited by at least four different colleges but didn't know which way to go. I just knew I needed to get away from home—I wanted something more for my life. I took the four-year scholarship with NCCU. I became an Eagle, but that didn't last long. Anytime there is no guidance, you are bound to keep repeating cycles. This was me, over and over. I kept making bad decisions, over which I'd cry over for days, weeks and sometimes even months.

While in college, I wanted to enjoy it, but there was still something missing. Being away from home for the first time. I was lonely. I didn't have nobody to talk to—where was my support system. I decided after my freshman year to leave and join the United States Army.

Being in the military, I was a proud soldier. I felt like I was doing something worthwhile. I liked having my own money. Coming from a place of poverty, to a solid stream of income, I felt like I'd made it big. Tears streamed down my face. I had no idea how I was going to tell my mother. I knew that she'd view this as another disappointment. A child was furthest from my mind. I was hurt, ashamed and disappointed. I was still dealing with the trauma of being violated at such a young age and I would soon be responsible for this innocent child. I wasn't sure I was ready for this. I had to decide if I should stay in the military or go home to my mother.

My first child was born, and while my life was forever changed; I was fighting to live due to a kidney infection which poisoned my entire system. I remember seeing my Mom beside my bed and family members with tears streaming down their face. I was transported to Chapel Hill Hospital, after Southeastern Regional could do nothing more. I spent 10 days in that hospital, dropping from 150 pounds to 101. One thing was clear. God was looking for me.

# CHAPTER 3

I HAD TO APPLY FOR WELFARE.

I knew after two months with receiving $232 monthly this wasn't for me. I got a job and worked until that factory closed. I never received another check from D.S.S. My baby was three months old, only to find out I was having my second. I was ashamed and embarrassed.

I had my second child and went back to work. I hoped their father would step up, but this hadn't happened. Things got worse. It started with him smoking marijuana and who knows what other drugs. Then the abuse started. If I didn't give him money, he would get angry and it would turn into physical or mental abuse. I tolerated it for years. He would do it and then apologize and I would forgive him and keep it moving.

The moment I discovered I was pregnant with my third child. I cried. I kept telling God, "I just can't do this. I can't go through this alone. I'm already taking care of two alone." Then there were the whispers and the gossip, but they didn't know the real deal. Every time I got pregnant; I was on birth control. The truth is that I never set out to have a baby—I just wanted to feel loved. I craved the emotional and physical intimacy that comes with loving and being loved.

The timing wasn't right for me to have another child. I just couldn't have this baby and this decision was a difficult one and it's haunted me for a long time. I was almost 25 years old and the mother of two children and pregnant with the third. I knew terminating the pregnancy was wrong—I felt it in my spirit, but I did what I knew to be the best thing for me. I often wondered what he or she would have been like. My children are amazing, and this one would have been too. Thoughts of the life I'd taken wouldn't let me forget or forgive myself.

I left the clinic with tears of pain and regret pouring down my face, asking myself why? No answer was good enough. This agony would be like driving nails in my heart, every time I thought about it. I didn't think I would ever be able to live with my decision.

I thought things would eventually go back to normal, but they never did. At this point in my life—I'd never felt so defeated. How in the world was I going to bounce back from the trauma stemming from the choice I'd made willingly? One that went against my personal belief system. How could I have allowed myself to get into such an emotionally draining situation? I worried that not even God would forgive my actions.

# CHAPTER. 4

I CONSTANTLY BEAT UP ON MYSELF ABOUT LEAVING THE MILITARY. ON the other hand, my Mom was diagnosed with colon cancer in 1992. I had the opportunity to spend the last six years of her life by her side. The year my mom was diagnosed with cancer, was the same year I gave birth to my second oldest daughter.

My third oldest sister was murdered on May 16, 1994. My body went completely limp when I was told about her death. The murder of my sister caused my mom's health to fail even the more. She couldn't even make the funeral. My mom died on my daughter's birthday less than six months later. I thought I would lose my mind. She was my support, and my sister moved every time I asked her. Now I was alone.

Two months later, my dad was diagnosed with cancer. I remember thinking I'm not built for this. It's just too much to bear.

I persevered, because giving up was not an option. I had others counting on me. I lost my identity while focusing on others. From 1995 to 2005, we were called multiple times to his bedside to decide whether to pull the plug or not. Each time he would bounce back. The last time the family was called in March 2005. Instinctively, I knew it would be the last time. Those were the best years of my life with my dad. We had an amazing relationship until his death. He became the father I'd always needed him to be and I cherish those memories to this day.

In May 2005, I was diagnosed with high blood pressure and several other health issues brought on by stress and not taking care of myself. All the losses I took had taken a toll on me mentally and physically. I didn't know how to release the anger and the bitterness that had formed in my heart. I'd tried so hard to be strong, until one day in the shower I broke. Both parents, the sister who was always there for me gone.

It was tragedy after tragedy.

Pain seemed almost second nature to me. But one day I realized that it was the foundation of my faith that kept me on top—faith is what always gave me a measure of hope that my beginning would not be my ending.

# CHAPTER 5

I WILL NEVER FORGET THE DAY I PICKED UP THE PHONE AND THE VOICE on the other end said, "Your son has been shot."

I will never forget when they pulled the cover back from his face, I hit the floor, his head was 3 times its size and I didn't recognize my baby laying on that gurney. He didn't die but the process of healing emotionally and physically had a devastating effect on me. Mentally I couldn't do it, but spiritually I was undergirded like never before. It was in this situation that my faith increased. However, there was one last event in my life that would sink me so low—I really didn't think I'd bounce back from it.

# CHAPTER 6

I REMEMBER ASKING MY PASTOR THIS QUESTION, "WHY DO I KEEP attracting the same type of men?" My first husband ended up on drugs. Same with the second marriage. I blamed myself for making such poor choices, but I needed to know why.

His answer was simple and straight to the point. "You don't value who you are."

I looked at him as if he'd grown two heads. I went home that night and for the next few days I began to ponder on those words. I was reminded how when my son was shot, the first person who walked back into my life was a young man who said all the right things, but he wasn't good for me. It's still too painful to talk about the why. Although I have forgiven him, the scars and the memories are still too raw. I was so weak-minded I thought that everybody would do right by you, especially if you're already hurting. I found out those are the times you are preyed upon.

I ignored the warnings. My relationship with my son went down the hill and I lost everything behind it. This brick wall woke me up.

It started with remembering who I really am. It wasn't predicated off someone else's love, it was predicated on how much I loved me. So, I began to clean out every closet of my life. Those that meant me no good, I began to cut. I disassociated myself with so many people. God took me down a path and it was very lonely for about three years.

I didn't get the phone calls, I didn't have people messaging me. I was beginning to think something was wrong with me. But this was the time my healing took place. My cargo was too precious to be contaminated ever again. Two failed marriages, sister murdered, mother and father gone, and my son shot. I focused on the positive not the negative. The Jericho experience began, and I am still in it. Greater is here and I am determined not to let my past ruin my future.

# AUTHOR BIO: NETTIE WILLIAMS

Nettie Williams is a single mom, all the way from Orrum North Carolina, by way of Long Island NY. She is the mother of four beautiful children and five amazing grandchildren. Nettie focuses daily on making sure she is an example of a Proverbs 31 woman for them.

She is a trendsetter and loves to encourage and push others to be successful. Her goal is to design a path for others to follow and do better than she had done. This is Nettie's first published work, and she prays her words will enable readers to tear down the walls within.

# IMPRISONED BY MY OWN CHAINS & FREED BY MY OWN WORDS

Tramaine McNeal-Wimbush

# CHAPTER 1

WHEN SOMEONE VIOLATES YOU AT AN AGE WHERE YOU'RE UNABLE TO defend yourself or fully understand what's going on, life can become a vicious cycle of victimization. You have no identity, other than being the receptacle for someone's lust, abuse or self-hatred. At the age of 13, I was raped by a boy who I thought was my boyfriend, who played me in order to get my goodies. At that time sex was never on my mind. I knew nothing about it, so I was clueless on the tricks and mind games that little boys like to play when it comes to wanting to have sex with a girl. In my parents' house boys and sex was not talked about. Once I went into one of my family members' dresser drawers, I found a small pink circle container and inside was what I assumed was tiny pieces of candy in a circle. I asked my mom for some and she said no and demanded that I put them back where I found them. When I was older in my adult age, I realized now that they were birth control pills.

Growing up all I heard was, "You don't do what I do—you do what I say do." I followed those instructions until I met this fine young boy named Dean. He was around 16 years old tall, slim with a Caramel complexion, short cut hair and brown eyes. He had on a white shirt and blue jean shorts. Before we started *dating*, I would see him around the neighborhood and in my mind, I would fantasize about being his girlfriend. Till one day he asked me if I had a boyfriend and of course I said no.

I'm not sure what made him seek me out, it's not like I was the prettiest girl in the neighborhood. But he asked me so I was down. All of this took place in the mid spring; one day my pager went off and it was him. His number appeared on the screen then I rushed to the phone to call him.

I did with a quickness.

He wanted to meet up so I asked, "Okay where?"

He gave me instructions to wait by a tree on the corner near the first apartment complex in my neighborhood.

I hung up the phone and headed out the door. I was so ecstatic the day had finally come to where I would get to hang out with my new boyfriend. There were so many thoughts running through my mind.

*Like what are we going to do?*

*What do I say? I couldn't believe this was really happening.*

Never in a million years would I have thought what was one of the happiest days in my life would take a turn for the worst. As I walked toward the corner, he was already there waiting for me.

"What are we going to do today?" I asked.

Dean responded, "I just want to talk and chill that's all."

We ended up at a mutual friend's house so I was cool with that.

Shortly after we got there, Dean called me into the bedroom.

"Why we can't stay in the living room?"

"I want to talk to you in private… just me and you."

I hesitated a moment before saying, "Okay, just for a little while, but not long because I don't like being in nobody's bedroom. Leave the door open."

As soon as I got into the bedroom the other boy turns and closed the door behind me. I quickly reached for the doorknob and attempted to push it back open. Dean quickly grabbed me and pushed me on the bed. The other boy on the outside of the door barricaded it with his weight.

Dean then proceeded to touch me. I screamed, hollered and told him I didn't want to do that. Stop! Stop! Stop it! I pushed him; even hit him, then he pinned me down onto the floor where I became powerless. I felt like it was over.

He won.

I went into a daze just to block out the pain. Yet I still felt myself squirming and crying yet powerless. My body became numb. I laid there until it was all over.

After Dean was done, I ran out of the house.

I was setup. But why and why me? I was in a state of shock; I didn't fully understand what had just happened. Until then I had kissed a boy a few times, but nothing like this. What made it so bad was it was one of the guys I trusted, a friend of my brothers and I had mixed emotions. I ran home showered and cried, scrubbed myself and cried, and scrubbed again. I was so hurt, and ashamed, I felt like it was entirely my fault. I knew better. I knew I should not have gone over there alone in the first place, but I did anyways. I blamed myself for years. I never told anyone what happened, and I never talked to that boy again.

# CHAPTER 2

As time went on it was soon summertime. You would've thought that I would have learned from the rape, but no I found myself in some more mess. I was introduced to another guy named Daniel by a friend of mine over the phone who changed my world upside down.

Daniel was the perfect gentleman he was 6 feet 1 inch tall with chocolate skin and brown eyes. Up until the time we met we would talk from sunup to sundown. I can even remember the nights we both fell asleep over the phone. I would be the one to wake up first and hear him breathing, his lips may have been slightly open as he inhaled and exhaled. After listening for a moment, calling his name softly and with no reply I simply hung up.

On a cool night while lying in my bed the phone lit up as colorfully as it rang, and it was Daniel.

He asked if I had wanted to meet him at a hotel party down on the oceanfront. I told him I wasn't the party type.

Daniel responded, "You are not here for the party you'll be here for me. I just want to see you."

I agreed to meet him, and he arranged for a ride to come and pick me up.

When we arrived at the hotel fear immediately gripped my heart just from the look of the exterior. Then entering the room I was over-taken by the smell of weed and cigarette smoke, reminding me of how just much I hate it.

As I was waded through the crowd; I asked a young man in passing, "Have you seen Daniel?"

He replied, "Yes he's over there."

I looked to my right and spotted him over by the turntable rapping with his homeboy Asher.

In the wee hours of that morning we left the party and took a walk on the beach. It was dark and chilly, yet peaceful.

I started to get cold and started shivering, so he gave me his jacket.

While we were walking we talked about his music and how he and homeboy wanted to become superstars. They had been selling their tapes for over a year at that time. We headed back to the room and talked some more.

Then he pulled out a blunt and asked me, "Do you smoke or drink?"

I said, "No."

"Good I don't think it looks good for a woman to do any one of those."

After that he asked if I could spend the night and even though I told him yes, I made it clear that I had to be home before seven a.m. I didn't want my dad to know I was out past curfew. At that time a nine p.m. curfew was the standard rule if were under the age of 18.

We went to sleep, and he held me the rest of the morning until it was time for me to go home. Just about every night I would sneak out the house after my father left to work. To get to the oceanfront; I would either walk or catch a ride to Virginia Beach after 11 p.m. at night. I would stay out until about five or six in the morning. From my house it was about a 20 minutes' walk or an 8 to 10 minute ride. Outside of going to church, the beach was another outlet for me.

I couldn't talk to my father, all he was going to do was preach Jesus to me. And I didn't want to hear anything about sin or how I was displeasing God. I just wanted the pain to go away. I already felt convicted over my actions and didn't need a reminder, so I would just go out walking or call a friend based on whatever mood I was in on that day, and that was the plan.

At the beach I loved the peaceful sound of the ocean and watching the currents in the ocean flow in and out of the sea. Depending on the time of the day or night I would just walk the strip. I used to love seeing the high-top cars with clearance lights blasting rap music or Reggae as they drove by. I had no worries just freedom, at least my definition of freedom.

———

ONE-NIGHT DANIEL CALLED AND ASKED IF I COULD MEET HIM AT THIS apartment off Virginia Beach Boulevard and of course I agreed.

I walked to the corner off the Boulevard and waited on his friend Asher to pick me up. When I got into the car Asher said, "Daniel told me to pick you up and he will meet us there. He had a few things to take care of."

Asher was always cool with people. He never said or did anything out of the way. I trusted him since Daniel and Asher were longtime friends.

However, when we arrived at the apartment, there were two other guys there that I'd never met before and no Daniel.

The hair on the back of my neck stood up and I felt uncomfortable. This scenario triggered my memory of the rape.

"Can you call Daniel and see where he is at?" I asked Asher.

He called. "D where you at man? Your girl is waiting for you."

I could hear Daniel's reply. "I'll be there in five minutes. Tell her not to leave."

I waited a little while, then I asked if I could use the restroom.

While I was making my way to the back one of the jokers who was in the apartment tried to make a pass at me.

"What are you doing? Stop it!"

I had to fight him off me. I yelled, "NO… NO… stop it. *Stop it*."

Asher came to my rescue. "Hey, what are you doing, man?"

"Ain't no woman going to come into my house and not give it up. She has got to go if she not giving it up."

I left.

As soon as I was outside, I started running down Virginia Boulevard as fast as I could, hoping with every step that he was not following me home. I cried and cried while in a state of disbelief. Why did this just happen again? That night literally changed my life as I finally slowed down to a walking pace.

I knew that I couldn't keep putting myself in these types of situations. I told myself that Daniel didn't love me because if he did—why didn't he show up? I knew I had to get myself together and leave those men alone.

But I really didn't know how to which clearly showed how naïve I was when it came to the things of the world. My solution was to stop hanging out with him altogether. Or shall I say just for a little while until he called me a few months later. It's like he had some type of spell on me that I couldn't break. Mind you I didn't miss him and I wasn't in love with him. He was just always there to listen to me whenever I needed him and that's what I loved the most. It was the attention that I lacked in my life. I knew he was poison I just had to find a cure, so I did.

What I ended up doing was getting more involved in church activities like singing in the choir. Getting involved in plays, I joined the step team even though I didn't have any rhythm. I created a whole new life for myself. Every time the church doors were open, I was there. I cried out to God and He helped me cope with everything I was dealing all those years. I constantly blamed myself for being raped. I would ask God to help me and keep me from these situations. Now I can admit to taking some responsibility. If I would have just talked to my father I would not have been looking for love in all the wrong places. We had always bumped heads, so I never knew what to say to him.

———

I ALSO CAME TO REALIZE THAT MY FATHER WAS DOING THE BEST THAT he could. He had grown up basically without a father in the home to pattern after. Therefore, he could only do what he knew and if I would have just obeyed his rules, I would have never gone through all of that.

I have an amazing dad who always provided for us; in fact, he worked two jobs. He was my protector and more. He laid down the rules and enforced them. He is a man after God's own heart, and he read to and taught us God's principles and he often reminded us we had to live by them. I was just one hardheaded little girl who wanted freedom or shall I say things her way more. I was either in church school or babysitting my twin brothers. Please don't mistake what I am saying. There are young women who need love from a father that is both strict and loving. I seemed to have gotten the strict disciplinary actions most of the time and less of the caring, loving father that I was longing for. I've enjoyed the time me and my father shared, but I knew there was more to life then praying all the time and reading bible stories at the dinner table.

The little girl in me still hurts at times, but with the help of the Lord in reading, believing and trusting in His words I know He can heal me from the inside out.

Since then I have discovered, I had been suppressing my feelings of things that had happened to me in my past, which caused a detour in my life and prevented me from moving forward later in life in my adulthood.

# CHAPTER 3

WE OFTEN SUPPRESS THE PAIN.

On November 2, 1997, at the age of 18, I got married and conceived my 3rd child.

My marriage as well as parenting my children was affected tremendously. In the First few months of our marriage everything was going well. We had our own place I was working part time for a short while at McDonalds. My husband was working two jobs and we didn't have to want for anything. I was in my last year of high school. I went to school during the day and on Tuesdays and Thursdays I went to night classes so I could graduate on time in June of 1998. I was so determined that I was not going to let anything hold me back from walking across that stage and receiving my high school diploma.

On graduation day, the ceremony was held at Roanoke Coliseum. I was so excited I forgot to invite anyone in fact it never even crossed my mind to tell my mom or dad. I was just glad that this stage of my life was over, and my diploma was my evidence.

My next thing on the list was college until a few people crushed that dream. The thing that was said to me was unbelievable. My best friend asked me, "Why you want to go? You don't have time for that." I had another lady tell me, "Well the field that you want to go into there is no money in it and you should change to something else. And how are you going to have time for studying when you have all young children in the home?"

After that I really didn't know what to do with my life. It was always a dream of mine to have my own business and make a lot of money. Yet nothing seemed to be working out. Why? Because I put my life in the hands of others and it led me nowhere, but minimum wage jobs or a stay at home mom. I began to get depressed and sad that my life was not going as planned and then on top of that one afternoon I was going through the closet being nosey, just looking for a few things that I noticed was missing of ours and I ran across a small black handbag.

When I looked inside, I almost lost my mind I mean literally felt a shift in my body. It was evidence that my husband had relapsed, and his drug of choice was crack cocaine. I immediately called on Jesus. I have never felt that feeling before and I don't ever want to feel that way again. Of course, he denied it when I asked. For a while things were okay until it got out of control then he wanted to move. So, we moved back to his hometown a place I had never been before. I hated it, I called it the city of dry bones it was so dead, boring and I felt so lonely. I really didn't know anyone which made it worse. I already had trust issues so now what. Our life was back to normal again once I found a church home to connect with. This was good for me because now I had an outlet. I would find myself talking to God and He would just download his revelation and knowledge to me.

One night He told me to read Jeremiah Chapter 1, verses 4-9:

*Then the word of the Lord came unto me, saying, Before I formed thee in the belly I knew thee; and before thou camest forth out of the womb I sanctified thee, and I ordained thee a prophet unto the nations.*

*Then said I, Ah, Lord God! Behold, I cannot speak: for I am a child.*

*But the Lord said unto me, Say not, I am a child: for thou shalt go to all that I shall send thee, and whatsoever I command thee thou shalt speak. Be not afraid of their faces: for I am with thee to deliver thee, saith the Lord. Then the Lord put forth his hand, and touched my mouth. And the Lord said unto me, Behold, I have put my words in thy mouth.*

I have always known God had a calling on my life as young as 11 years old. I was never taught the process that you have to go through to do his will. At that point I believed my relationship with Him was sharp and you couldn't tell me nothing otherwise.

Until I was faced with another problem then I was back at the drawing board trying to figure out what to do now. I thought I had fixed all my issues, but things began to surface and started causing problems in my home life. Particularly with intimacy; my husband wanted to make love more often than I desired.

"Sex just isn't my thing anymore." I used to tell him. "Well, is there anything else we can do besides that? I'm getting tired of always pleasing you, what about my needs?" It had even gotten to the point where I wouldn't even get undressed in front of him and when I did, I would cover my body parts and the lights always had to be off. I was acting shy, insecure, ashamed and embarrassed and I couldn't explain why because even I didn't know. Yet regardless of how I was feeling I would do whatever he asked just to keep the peace in our home. On the days I refused to sleep with him, we would have heated discussions, which led me to pray to God often to help me in this area, time and time again. I loved my husband and would give him the world and even though I was present physically I wasn't present emotionally and he knew it.

———

I SEARCHED FOR A SOLUTION BY TALKING TO OTHER FIRST LADIES whom I trusted. I listened to podcasts, praise and worship music, read books, watched YouTube videos, and attended marriage seminars. I wanted my marriage to work.

One night we were laying in bed talking about life and I decided to discuss with him some things that had taken place in my life when I finally realized the strongholds which had me bound. I was so grateful that my husband not only listened, but he understood. We can be our own worst enemy, but that can change only when we take action.

Change didn't take place for me overnight. My last straw was years and I mean years down the line when my husband accepted the call to be a pastor which made me a First Lady. Through the nine years of being the First Lady, I was mostly missing in action. I went to church whenever I felt like it, that's how bad I was hurting on the inside. I felt like I was unwanted there most times.

The role of a First Lady is not an easy role in fact I lost myself completely during the process. I was told I wasn't doing enough, or you are going to run people away being so hard on them. I was called bougie because of how I carried myself or how I dressed, and I was standoffish.

I was even chastised for giving the Leader good advice on some of the situations that was going on in the church. I love God's people and always wanted what was best for them and to see them walk in the calling that God has placed in them. I believe strongly in unity for where there is unity there is strength. We need each other in order to get to the next level in life. I ended up becoming a people pleaser and didn't even know it. I was thinking maybe I am the problem; maybe I should spend more time with the people. Maybe I should call them more. Then over time it all became overwhelming and one night during praise and worship I told the church that in the coming year it was going to be all about me.

However, I have to do what God has called me to do, but what I was really saying was I have to find me again and take care of home.

There are times in our lives when we have to deal with the truths about ourselves in order to be healed from it. Self-discovery is very important in order to move on. Because in this journey called life you have to first know who you are and where you are headed. God spoke these words to me from the book of Habakkuk 2:2: *Write the vision, and make it plain on tablets, that he may run who reads it.*

# CHAPTER 4

My husband was patient when I asked him to please give me some time to work on the issue that had disrupted our intimacy. I reassured him that it had nothing to do with him. That it was the flashbacks that were coming back to me each time he would touch me. He understood and we began to make plans together on how to improve things in our life throughout my healing process. I would often quote this Bible verse from Philippians 4:13: *I can do all things through Christ which strengthens me.*

I knew I didn't have the strength to do it on my own. Christ was my lifeline I don't know where I would have been without him.

I had to conclude that I was going to break free from the prisoner within; if I wanted to live a holistic life, it was up to me. I hold the keys to my own freedom and God gave me this word in 3 John 2:2: *Beloved I wish above all things that thou mayest prosper and be in good health, even as thy soul prospereth.*

What I did was I started with the mind I had to think about what I was thinking about. I held on to every word that was spoken over my life I had my own personal tape recorder playing in mind day in and day out. Proverbs 18:21 says, *death and life are in the power of the tongue: and they that love it shall eat the fruit thereof.*

Everything that existed in my life at that present moment I spoke it, believed it, I received it, and I lived it until it became my lifestyle. I had to take the power back over my mind and my thoughts and even the very words that I spoke into the atmosphere. I became very conscious of where I went or who was talking to me in this season of my life. I put myself through a spiritual, emotional, and mental surgery. Only the words that were sent by God were allowed in the room— meaning in my life. I looked myself in the mirror and said, "Tramaine, it's time that you take your power back you have been giving it way for so long and to so many people. Don't worry about what they say or how they feel. For people are entitled to their own opinion. What God has for you it is for you and He has already spoken over your life you just now have to walk it out and live. Live your life and not another."

This is what I told myself for months as often as I needed to until I was strong enough. Now I can tell them the truth with no problem when I am asked or when something is said or done. Every day is a war, but I am glad because I can see the growth in me and I can now deal with any obstacle that comes my way. Now some stuff tries to hit me hard like a confrontation or in a meeting with someone. Before, I would run from it at all costs or just let you win the whole case and be done. I had to change that because the problem was not solved and it showed I still had some residue left over from my past. Therefore, I needed some help so I called on my Savior and this is what He said me: Philippians 4:13 says, *I (Tramaine) can do all things through Christ who strengthens me.*

I needed someone more powerful than how I was feeling at that moment to handle this situation or any situation I might encounter until I am able to stand alone with Him leading me. Apart from God He has placed some amazing people in my life that has helped me along this journey in so many ways when it comes to living life full circle. All I had to do was put some action behind my faith for faith without works is nothing but dead faith. I had the faith and the tools to advance but not the works. I was so afraid of what was going to be said about me or if they would accept the real me. I would tell myself well you don't look the part you need to lose weight or your need a face lift and the list goes on and on.

However, today is a new day and I'm so grateful that in October of 2018 I was introduced to SRT Global Academy which teaches people about how to deal with the Subconscious mind. After the first lesson I was hooked. Everything that I needed to bring total restoration was in this Academy.

Then a few months later, Tonya and Dexter Scott who had introduced me to SRT Global had made mention to me about the crazy confidence course before it launched. Of course, I jumped on it and signed up for the 30-day program which changed my life completely. I had hope again and I could now see the light at the end of the tunnel. My husband and I are living our best life. We are both free from our past to God be the Glory. My children are getting back on the right track.

You have the power on the inside to be and do what you have in your heart. You are more than a conqueror and remember these two powerful words **I Am**. You are what you speak. So, speak your truth: I am powerful, I am strong, I am wealthy, and I am healthy and the list can go on and on.

At this time in my life I am now unapologetic with the choices that I make. I had to learn me all over again and take actions. It feels good to be free and it's not over yet. I am now able to help others live the life that is already theirs. I have always known that the battle was already won; I just had to believe it receive it and walk it. Finally, I now keep a forgiving heart. Forgiveness is not for the other person it's for you. I am healthier and the stress levels in my body are back to normal. I am forming newer and better relationships in my business and personal life. The best is here and is still yet to come now that I realize I hold the keys to my own freedom.

It's now time for you to take hold of your keys. To live and be the best servant for the Lord, the best wife, mother, coach, business owner or partner that God has chosen you to be. Freedom is already yours now live it and walk in your victory.

# AUTHOR BIO: TRAMAINE MCNEAL-WIMBUSH

Tramaine Wimbush is the CEO and Founder of Full Circle Life Coaching. She is also the first Lady at God's House of the Remnant. For over 20 years, Tramaine has helped many women break free from being a prisoner within, and not only has she helped women stop being a slave to their own thoughts.

Tramaine has also reinforced the importance of living full circle in the mind, body and soul. The strategics that she used has not only set her clients free—she is free from bondage by applying these methods to her own life. She has helped women reclaim their power back by first identifying where they are in their current state. Her ultimate goal is to help women live their life full circle.

# KUTTIN WEIGHT

## Kimberly Mills

# CHAPTER 1

## Dead Woman Walking

You wake up and go about your normal Saturday morning routine, folding clothes when you're suddenly slapped in the face by the terse announcement that your husband never wanted the responsibility of a house and family. It's like you're living in the twilight zone. You invest nearly 12 years with a man who suddenly decides to confess he never really wanted to be with you.

When I inquired as to why he married me, his response was, "Because you will work."

Needless to say, this was a blow I didn't expect. I think I knew all along that he didn't love me because his actions indicated this truth, but hearing the words come out of his mouth—my heart didn't just break. It shattered into millions of little pieces that would forever leave holes, not only in my heart, but in my soul.

His words cut deep, but they were exactly what I needed to wake up. For years, I'd ignored my goals and dreams—everything that God had instilled in me. I allowed my marriage to kill my spirit. I knew I had to make some changes starting with me.

It took three years for me to heal from the heartbreak and for the heat of my anger to burn down. I learned how to channel the energy to fuel me for better. I learned to forgive myself for not loving me more than I loved my ex-husband. I found a love for HIIT (High Intensity Interval Training) I found my love for reading again, I found a love for my children without the hurt attached. But before I could get to this point—I was a dead woman walking.

# CHAPTER 2

## Self-Preservation

I WAS ALWAYS DEFENSIVE BECAUSE I WANTED TO PROTECT MYSELF. Always felt as if I had to be on guard and this didn't allow me to see life, it didn't allow me to live. This all began because of the missing elements needed during the early stages of my life. There was never a time I can recall that my talents or dreams were nurtured; they were always dismissed as me being crazy or having an unrealistic imagination. This caused me to turn to food to help comfort those emotions of feeling inadequate. I never realized this until I was 35 years old. I no longer wanted to live in bondage to my past hurts, so I decided to seek professional help.

My search helped me discover some of the myths I had allowed myself to believe. I worked jobs for 20 plus years because I was told this is what we are supposed to do once we become adults. I wasn't told you are to discover the talents God gave you and work towards bettering His Kingdom with your talents. I was held hostage to what others thought to be right for my life. This caused me to eat even more. I would sit and eat to avoid conversations with people. I would decline invites or not show up to events to avoid the stares people would give me because of my weight. I was told I should be embarrassed to go to the vending machine at work because of my weight. All these things combined with hearing I was a bastard hundreds of times as a child, all of these elements and layers created the dead woman walking. I became numb on the inside; numb to the true desires I wanted for my life.

Food was my best friend for 30 plus years. I would often try to justify what was happening by looking at myself in the mirror and I would say, "No matter how big you get, I will always love you."

The truth was that I was killing myself.

If there was a new food on the market I felt it to be my duty to the "FAT GIRL" in me to try it and give my review. I thought people would like me if I would tell them about a great food. These are the types of lies I was telling myself for years. I would rationalize why I didn't want to acknowledge that I needed a change, not to acknowledge I was the walking dead. I let everything, and anything determine who or what I was, and food allowed me to sink into a state of depression that only I knew existed. I can recall times I would go to the corner store and purchase a bag of candy then come home and lie on my bed and eat every single piece of candy while drinking Dr. Pepper and smoking Newport's. I did this every Friday night for years.

This was my way to unwind after working so hard at nothing to improve myself all week. I would fool myself into thinking that Monday's were always the starting point to me changing my eating habits. The hard fact was that I would wake up Monday morning with the intent not to eat horrible; then stop by Bojangles on the way to work and say, "Oh, this one meal will not kill me." However, it was killing me because it caused me to crave the Bojangles or whatever fast food I chose even more. I didn't allow the God within to guide me. I allowed the words and comments of others to make me sink deeper within my walking dead self.

Much of this goes back to me when I was as young as 10 years old playing with family members and hearing the adults talk about my weight, comparing me to the other children my age. Some adults wouldn't allow me to go places with them because I was an embarrassment to them and little did they know I could hear what they were saying. Things like this caused me to resent them but as a child I didn't have a choice. Those early childhood experiences are the reason why now I'm so cautious about what I say and do with children. Words said to a child at an early age can scar their emotions and psyche within them for life. I can recall one incident that occurred when I was playing with my family members while my mother was attending a funeral.

The babysitter wanted to go to the mall and took the other children in the house and cleaned them up. We all were playing in the dirt, so you know how children look dusty and dirty when they have been playing outside all day. I was taken to my mother without being cleaned and dropped off at the cemetery. Now, I didn't know if the adult was upset with my mother or they just didn't like me as a child. As a child, I didn't deserve to not have my face cleaned before being dropped off. I can still see the dingy white shirt and green shorts I was wearing that day. I can still see me standing in front of my mom and she not saying a thing when the other adult said, "Here's your child. I'm going to the mall." While it may seem small to some, this was huge to me because this same adult often would call me a bastard child. I remember having to ask my mother what it meant.

She explained because she wasn't married to my father I was considered a bastard. Do you know the scars this can leave on a child? The only thing that didn't hurt me was food. Food was my ever present friend and it comforted me. I thought I could eat until I didn't feel the hurt anymore until the next time someone would do the same to me. Episodes like this would continue to happen for years and I was always told I had a bad attitude.

Yes, I did have a bad attitude because what they didn't know was that as I grew older I knew the conversations that were being had about me, but I was still too young to have my voice heard. No matter what I did or would do to keep myself safe I was pushed down, I was never encouraged, I was always told what I was going to be... nothing.

This same adult told me as I graduated high school I was not going to be anything and that I would just lay up on my momma and have babies. It was at that time I knew they hated me as a person because who would tell a child that just received their high school diploma they weren't going to amount to anything. This same adult told me at the age of 21 they hated me as child. While those words hurt and caused me to wonder what I'd ever done to that person—I no longer care. The chains that once held me in bondage over the words cast in meanest are gone. I am FREE.

You see, I believe what the Lord says about me. I believe who He says I am—He calls me daughter. He loves me. I believe Him. The words of others—they are just that, some motivated by their own personal demons—it is not my battle or responsibility to try and figure out the nature of other folks actions and behaviors. However, it is my choice to remove all toxic relationships from my life while working to be the best version of myself.

# CHAPTER 3

## The Transformation Begins

IN 2011, I BEGAN MY JOURNEY TO A BETTER ME. THE FIRST CHANGE was to stop smoking cigarettes which led to leaving sodas alone. I knew if I could stop smoking I could stop the cycle of abuse I was enforcing on myself living in my past. Though I stopped smoking I didn't stop eating, so my weight got out of control. I remember the scale saying 279 pounds and I vowed I would never see 300 pounds.

I never saw 300 pounds but in my heart of hearts I believe I reached that number, but I refused to weigh myself. Refusing to weigh myself and avoiding difficult conversations and difficult situations is what got me living like the walking dead. I didn't like myself, I didn't love myself, I didn't like anything about my life. I was miserable. I would go to work daily and, on the way home each day, I would say this is not what God wants for my life. He doesn't want me working for anyone. He wants me to do what He's told me all my life. I always have had a desire to help people, but I had to help myself first.

At first, I didn't think God loved me because how could he allow these things to happen to me. When in fact I began to realize that I had allowed these things to happen because I didn't speak up for myself. Why wasn't I able to control my weight? Why wasn't I able to rid myself of the judgements? Why did it matter what happened to me when I was a child? Why, just why was I not able to live the way I envisioned? Why?

I had to sit down and really take a deep look at me. I had to invest the time to truly admit what I wanted and acknowledge what was always in me. I just had to look within and begin to tap into my greatness. I started out simply. I would lay on my bed and envision what life would be like when I reached my goal of being healthy. I envisioned myself and what I looked like, what it felt like and how it truly would feel to be the healthiest person in the room. I would tell myself you already know what it feels like to be the unhealthiest why don't you push to be the healthiest. Then I started pushing myself. I would make myself no matter how late it was when I got home I would walk two miles. During those walks I would talk to myself and tell myself I can do it, if I did it yesterday I can do it again today. I pushed and lost 29 pounds.

I got so excited and somewhat blinded by my progress that I told myself I could start back eating the way I was eating before and still lose weight. When I woke up and realized what I had to done to myself I knew it was time for something drastic, so I decided to have weight loss surgery.

# CHAPTER 4

## Transfer Addiction after Surgery

July 17, 2013 is the day I had my surgery—I was reborn. However, my struggles didn't end there. When I was no longer able to eat comfort foods, I turned to marijuana. I kept the people around me that smoked and would validate smoking was okay; trying to reinforce the thoughts that marijuana wouldn't hurt me.

I thought it was okay until I realized I was craving weed like I had craved for sweets. I had to make a change. I didn't want to seek professional help because I knew this time it was an inside job. I'd transferred from food to marijuana because I was not dealing with my internal issues. When I say kuttin weight, it's not just a physical cut. It's emotional, mental, and people as well. I had to re-evaluate everyone and everything in my life. I was so unhappy and miserable within myself that this is what I had attracted into my life. I had to step back and look at how I was showing up in my own life. If I wasn't giving myself the best version of myself, how could I expect anyone else to care about me.

I thought having weight loss surgery would change my life in all areas, but this wasn't realistic. I had to grow into the person that I desired from the inside.

# CHAPTER 5

## Life Changing Morning

ONE MORNING I WOKE UP AND FELT A SHIFT IN MY LIFE. I SAT ON THE side of my bed and broke down in tears. I couldn't understand why after I had done all this work to improve myself and I still wasn't accepted by my current circle. That's the day I realized I was in the wrong circle and needed to remove myself from their influence. It wasn't the easiest thing for me to walk away from everyone and what had become my comfort zone, but it was one of the best decisions I've ever made for myself. I realized to live the life I desire I had to surround myself with the things that would push me to be better.

Carrying around the burden of wanting to be accepted is a burden I no longer wished to carry. I despised hearing people talk about other people. I chose to stop allowing those type of people into my circle.

# CHAPTER 6

## Being the Change I Want to See

I DECIDED DURING MY PROCESS THROUGH WLS I WOULD CHANGE HOW I viewed the world and lead with love. I will not say it's been easy at all, but it has truly been rewarding. I've started to see people in a different light. Now those who aren't an influence for making me better I am able to walk away from them easily.

I'm no longer afraid to dive into the deep end of life and explore all God has created. It is my hope that we all are working to discover what God has instilled in us. I want to encourage others to begin to help themselves see that life is to be lived abundantly and free from the weights that can so easily trap and trip us up. Life can be fun and it's a journey we all have a right to discover and my prayer is we all find it within ourselves to live it. I awake every day with joy in my heart, looking forward to seeing my granddaughter every day looking forward to her smile. I have promised her that the same people that hurt me will not hurt her, I will instill all I've learned into her, so she will be able to live the life she desires…the life God has promised us all.

WLS has been the vehicle I needed to discover me. My goals now are to help as many people as possible discover life after weight loss surgery.

# CHAPTER 7

## Kuttin Weight

WHAT KUTTIN WEIGHT HAS MEANT TO ME IS THE PROCESS OF FINALLY getting rid of everything from my past. I hope that by sharing my story, others will be inspired and motivated to *kut the weight* out of their lives too. I want to show them that what we imagine in our minds eye, we can hold in our hand. These are the things God has promised us.

After all that has happened, I boldly step into my greatness. And I encourage you to step into yours too!

# AUTHOR BIO: KIMBERLY MILLS

KIMBERLY MILLS WILLIAMS IS THE mother of two children and the grandmother of one. She has worked in corporate America for many years before deciding in 2014 to pursue her desire to help others create a healthier lifestyle.

She is also on a journey to better health and wellness. Kimberly is constantly searching for ways to improve her mind, body and soul. She has a love for learning new strategies that will enable her to improve personally and professionally.

Kimberly is originally from Kinston, NC but currently resides in Raleigh with her children.

# AFTERWORD

## Latesha Williams

*She made struggle look like strength...*
*the way she broke through barrier after barrier...*
*stopping only to catch her breath...*
*replenish on the word... the word of God which sounded*
*    like FAITH... TRUST... LOVE...*
*she pushed forward... losing weight, those no longer*
*    needed, along the way...*
*her tears bathed her... rinsing away the dirt that once*
*    stained her... shedding dead skin... healing old*
*    wounds... ones she'd played in too long... leaving*
*    scars and bruises...*
*that was then she said... as the sun rose over new*
*    horizons... each rise shedding light on a new day...*
*a new day to forgive... to obey... to pray for God's will...*
*    to lead her when others tried to lead her astray...*
*she made struggle look like STRENGTH*

Made in the USA
Monee, IL
25 January 2020

20875794R00206